A Stolen Childhood

CASEY WATSON

A Stolen Childhood

A dark past, a terrible secret, a girl without a future

HARPER
element

This book is a work of non-fiction based on the author's experiences.
In order to protect privacy, names, identifying characteristics,
dialogue and details have been changed or reconstructed.

HarperElement
An imprint of HarperCollins*Publishers*
1 London Bridge Street
London SE1 9GF

www.harpercollins.co.uk

First published by HarperElement 2015

1 3 5 7 9 10 8 6 4 2

A catalogue record of this book is
available from the British Library

PB ISBN 978-0-00-754309-0
EB ISBN 978-0-00-811862-4

Printed and bound in Great Britain by
Clays Ltd, St Ives plc

MIX
Paper from
responsible sources
FSC **FSC™ C007454**
www.fsc.org

*Some wise person, somewhere, coined the phrase,
'It's the little things,' and you know, it really is.
This book is dedicated to all those who do the little things
without thinking, every working day. The dinner ladies,
the playground assistants, the volunteer mentors and the
teachers, the classroom assistants, the school nurses,
the year heads and the support staff. These people, in
their dedicated roles and in the busy school environment,
often have no idea what a positive effect they have on
their students. Continue doing what you do, and know
that every little smile you give, every pat on the back,
every wink or nod in the corridor, really makes
somebody's day. I raise a glass to all of you.*

Acknowledgements

I would like to thank my agent, the lovely Andrew Lownie, for continuing to believe in me; Carolyn and the wonderful team at HarperCollins for their dedicated and hard work; and as ever my very talented friend and mentor, Lynne, for always being there.

Chapter 1

What Lies Beneath. That was the name of the film, wasn't it? The one where the wife thinks she's seeing things that aren't there? As titles went, it was a good one for a psychological thriller. But though it would soon strike a chilling chord with me for professional reasons, right now I was oblivious of what lay in store, so it came to mind for more practical ones. I was busy digging – digging deep into my capacious school satchel, to see if what lay beneath in this case was a pen that actually worked.

It was touch and go whether I'd have any success. In fact, it was an action that, at times, put me in mind of one of those celebrities in the jungle plunging a hand into a black hole while being blindfold. It was a very big satchel and there was a great deal of stuff generally at the bottom of it, which was par for the course given the nature of my job. 'You know what?' I said to Kelly, my sometime assistant, having turfed out half the contents in order to find one, 'you would think that after all this time, someone would finally work out how to operate the heating system in this place, wouldn't you? It's not exactly rocket science, after all.'

It was mid-morning break and Kelly and I, along with a lot of the other teaching staff, were spending it in the staff-room – not just so we could warm ourselves up a bit with hot drinks, but so we could retrieve any extra clothing we might have in our lockers.

It was only the beginning of March, but it was almost as if all the radiators in the place somehow knew that the weathermen had announced that morning that it was officially the first day of spring. They had then apparently decided in unison that they should break down, quite possibly for the entire season. This in turn meant that the school was already going into the usual 'cold weather meltdown', with key staff bustling about the place bearing thermometers and recording temperatures, while the children – always quick to sniff an opportunity on the breeze, particularly a chilly one – could already be heard up and down the corridors making plans for a possible early exit, if there were insufficient degrees Celsius for them to be allowed to stay.

'It's not boiler science either,' Kelly told me. 'Not on this occasion, anyway. I just saw Donald on the way up here and he said it's not the boilers. Apparently someone turned the whole system off over the weekend by mistake and it's just taking a long time to kick in again. Still,' she said, grabbing a biscuit from the half-opened packet on the table in front of us, 'didn't Ranulph Fiennes say that when it's really cold you burn loads of extra calories through shivering? So that's fine by me. Custard cream?'

Her enthusiasm for trying to force-feed me biscuits aside, Kelly Vickers was a godsend in my working life. One of the school's 20 or so teaching assistants, she was assigned, first and foremost, to help me as and when required in my role as the school's Behaviour Manager. Ours was a busy inner-city comprehensive, big enough to have a specialised behaviour unit (well, to us, just 'the Unit') where my job was all about helping the various children who, for one reason or another, couldn't cope effectively in mainstream classes. It was a veritable 'mixed bag' of reasons, as well, including children who were in danger of being excluded, those who had problems in school (be they academic and/ or social) and kids who were struggling because of problems at home – something that naturally tended to impact on a child's progress and well-being.

The diversity of my pupils' needs meant that no day was ever just like another and, unlike most of the mainstream teachers, who had clear curriculum-based briefs, I couldn't plan too far ahead because I never knew from one day to the next just who I might have in my classroom.

Today, though, I was completely child-free. 'Well, I hope they sort it out soon,' I said, declining the proffered biscuit packet and reaching for my coffee, 'or we'll have a hard time engaging our new brood tomorrow, won't we? I don't think there's anything moodier than a kid that's too hot or too cold.'

Kelly nodded as she cupped her own plastic vending-machine cup. 'Have they told you who's coming in yet?'

I shook my head. What with all the kerfuffle over the heating, my scheduled meeting with Julia Styles, the school's Special Educational Needs Co-ordinator (or SENCO) had been knocked off the morning's agenda. 'No names, no pack drill, not as yet,' I told her. 'All I know is that there are three of them – a lad from year seven, another from year eight and a girl from year nine with long-standing learning difficulties. I'm hoping to get more up to speed on them later on today.'

'I tell you what,' Kelly said, 'I think I know who the girl might be. I remember someone mentioning to me she was joining the unit when you came back. If it's the one I'm thinking of, her name's Chloe Jones. Mother's a long-standing alcoholic and social services are heavily involved with them, though as far as I know there are no plans to place her in care. There *are* moves afoot, however, to try and get Chloe moved out of mainstream education. She can be difficult to keep an eye on, bless her.'

'How do you mean?' I asked, having had my fair share of serial absconders since working at the school. 'You mean she runs off all the time?'

Kelly shook her head. 'No, not that – it's more that she's rather vulnerable, particularly now she's an adolescent; tends to put herself in potentially dangerous situations. She has this thing where she wants to hug and kiss almost everyone. She automatically assumes that everyone loves her. The other kids tease her mercilessly and she believes anything they tell her. You'll love her though, Casey, if it is her. She's so adorable.'

'Well, that's always a bonus,' I said. 'I'd much prefer a surfeit of hugs than tantrums and rages. And I guess we'll see what we'll see come the morning. Right now I'm looking forward to a bit of peace and quiet in that classroom of mine.' I picked up the piece of paper I'd been scribbling on before my pen gave up the ghost. 'And a little light shopping from the stationery catalogue. You know me – I do like to be organised to a fault.'

'Well, you know where I am if you need a hand in the morning,' Kelly said as we gathered our things together. 'You know, to help settle them in, whoever they turn out to be. Just give me a buzz and I'll be there. I'm only helping out in the learning support room for the rest of the week, and at the moment there are more staff than children. 'Oh, and Casey,' Kelly added, grinning, as I slung my satchel over my shoulder, 'remember Baden-Powell!'

'Baden Powell? I don't get you.'

She handed me a nail file, a packet of tissues, my purse and some lip balm. 'Yours, I think?' she added, with a mocking salute. 'Be prepared!'

Only in schools, I mused as I walked the chilly corridors on the well-trodden route to my classroom. In no other job I could think of did you hear about all the staff being sent home because the temperature had dropped by just a few degrees. A great occasion for most of the children, no doubt about it, but not so much for teachers, some of whom had travelled miles to get to work, and definitely not

5

for working parents who would have to quickly arrange transport and unexpected childcare.

Hopefully the radiators would chunter into life before it came to that, and we could all warm up and get to grips with the day. Not that I imagined I'd be cold for long as I had lots of physical work to be doing before welcoming my new brood to the Unit. I unlocked the door and opened it onto the cold, empty room, which smelt faintly musty from its long period unused. Since coming back to school after Christmas, I had had an unusual sort of term; one where I hadn't really had the usual set group to work with. Only three kids from the previous term had returned to me after the holidays: Gavin and Shona, who'd both returned to mainstream classes by mid-January, and Imogen, a girl who'd had selective mutism and had come to us from another school, and who was settled into a new class by the end of the month. Since then the Unit had been temporarily de-commissioned, as I'd been working away from the main school, helping set up a new off-site facility that would deliver a brand new teaching programme.

It had been a big project, led by our visionary head-teacher, Mike Moore, and enthusiastically supported by our Child Protection Officer, Gary Clark. Called 'Reach for Success' it was the culmination of research, endless meetings, and lots of political toing and froing with the education authorities, most of which I wasn't personally involved with, but some of which I was, and we were now the proud 'owners' of a dedicated teaching facility in the local youth centre. It was designed to bring out the potential of a specific group of children – those who would not, in all probability, achieve academically in the same way as the majority of the kids.

It was an important step, not least because it meant we could target those kids that might leave school feeling academic 'failures' but were of course supremely capable of succeeding beyond school, and deliver an alternative and more appropriate teaching programme for them, including cookery, health and social care, basic food hygiene, child-care, beauty and more manual training in mechanics and carpentry than they could get in the main school. It was to be delivered as a rolling six-week course of learning exciting new, career-focused skills, and would also include targeted work on behaviour and self-development, which was where I came in, of course. I'd also had to provide the teaching staff down there with some specific agendas, which could be implemented during timetabled lessons.

All the hard work now completed, and the key staff in place, we were almost 'open for business', as it were. All that remained for me to do was to help identify the first group of pupils that we would send on the programme, make a weekly visit to the centre to check on their progress, and keep teachers and parents in the loop about how each individual was performing. It was a really exciting and innovative development for our school and I was proud of how much we'd achieved in a relatively short space of time.

It had been a pretty full-on job over the past few weeks, as well. So much so that it meant that I had spent even less time at home with my husband Mike and my own two children. Who weren't exactly children any more, to be fair. Riley, my daughter, was almost 19 now, and my son Kieron had just turned 17, though sometimes, when I came home after a physically exhausting day spent painting and decorating at the centre, you'd think they *were* kids. I'd more than once come in to find the house in complete chaos – which I hated – and to find two starving teenagers and a husband with a hangdog expression, all obviously of the opinion that a law had been passed forbidding them to eat until I arrived home.

Not that it wasn't a situation of my own making. I might stomp about a bit, do a lot of martyred sighing and so on, but that didn't mean I was blind to my own failings. In fact, it often amused me that I spent all day teaching other people's kids how to look after themselves, only to then go home and insist on doing absolutely everything for my own.

'You're making a rod for your own back, Casey!' my mother was rather fond of saying, and even though I'd huff and puff at her, I was inclined to agree. Not that I'd have it any other way of course. I secretly loved still being needed by my two older teens, no matter how much I pretended to protest.

Right then, Casey, I said out loud to myself, since there was no one else to talk to. *Best get cracking – these walls aren't going to sort themselves out!* I then rolled my sleeves up, both actually and metaphorically, and, after placing a hopeful hand on the nearest radiator and having my hopes dashed, prepared to do battle with the displays. With any luck, I'd have an uninterrupted hour and a half now, so, before tackling the remaining backlog of paperwork in my pigeonhole, I could do a good job of stripping down all the previous students' work, and prettying it up again, ready for the work my new charges would produce.

But that's the thing about school life; it was almost always unpredictable. So much so that I could probably have predicted that the sudden rap on the classroom door 20 minutes later would mean a complete change of plan.

And it did.

Chapter 2

My room wasn't like a regular classroom. For one thing it was half the size, and for another, it wasn't even a classroom. It had been once, back in the dark ages, when the school had first been built, but after a spell as a learning support room, it had gone the way of many a backwater space – home to a small, motley collection of tables and chairs, and not a great deal else. It had been passed over, forgotten, trapped in a time warp at the end of a corridor, and it suited my purposes perfectly.

The headmaster, Mike Moore, who showed me various options when I'd first secured the job, had expressed surprise; in terms of size and spec he'd definitely shown me better. But there was something about that little room that had chimed with my sensibilities, both as a work space for me and as a safe space for my pupils – who I had an inkling would know all about being passed over and forgotten.

Best of all – and, to be honest, it was probably the deal-breaker – it had double doors that opened out onto a lovely grassy area, tucked away at the back of the school. Oh, the things we could do out there, I'd thought.

And, if I did say so myself, I thought I'd made it quite special. I sectioned off an area at the front for myself, which contained a desk, a set of drawers and (important, to my mind) space to make hot drinks and toast. This last addition had caused a few raised eyebrows. In these days of health and safety consciousness, one couldn't just turn up and plug in a toaster as one might do at home – no, Mike Moore had been required to call an engineer in specially, to test and 'pass safe' my two electrical appliances, which I heard on the grapevine caused a ripple of mild disgruntlement in some quarters, due to the 'unnecessary' expense.

I believe I then made matters worse (no, to be fair, I know I did) by going out and spending some of my precious teaching budget on such fripperies as bright emulsion, half a dozen floor cushions and a selection of potted plants – all of which I deemed essential too. Essential to the creation of the warm, calm environment I was after, so, knowing all about politics after years spent working with vulnerable young adults for the local council, I simply ignored the whispered grumbles and exasperated glances, which, once it became common knowledge that my Unit would mop up the most challenging children, did not continue very long, to no one's surprise.

I had several large display boards and had got to work on them quickly, taking down what remained of the previous bunch of students' work and, while I was at it, wondering how they were all doing. Being out of school for a few weeks meant being somewhat out of the loop, and I made a mental note to try and track them down when I could. In the meantime, I decided, surveying the newly barren walls, I'd hang on to the gold card frames that we'd put up for Christmas but would be perfectly serviceable for a while yet. I could then turn my attention to my 'quiet' area.

A good number of the children who came to me had a tendency to become volatile, so a 'chill out' space was another essential. It was a place I could send kids to calm down if they needed to and, equally, it was a place that might prove preventative on that front – not to mention being somewhere a shy child could escape to, should the bustle of the classroom get too much.

It was a simple space – the only seating being those half-dozen floor cushions – and bound on two sides by a pair of bookcases at right angles, facing inwards. There were books, of course, but also a selection of stationery: trays of paper, pens and pencils, in case creativity blossomed and the urge to be artistic took hold.

The knock at my door came just as I was deciding if I had time to rearrange the muddle of books, while putting a new label on the crayon tray. I bobbed up to find Donald Brabbiner, the deputy head, had put his head round the now open door.

'Casey, do you have a minute?' he asked, looking stressed. Not that Don looking stressed was anything unusual in itself, currently. The school was in the middle of preparing for an OFSTED visit, and there wasn't a member of the senior staff who *wasn't* stressing about it – the furrowed brow and frazzled expression was very much the look of the moment.

But, no – he looked more stressed than even that, I decided. 'Yes, of course, Don,' I said, pulling myself upright and brushing chalk dust from my skirt. 'I don't have any children in till tomorrow, and I'm about done here. Is there a problem?'

He nodded grimly. 'Apparently so.'

He was obviously keen to return to it, too, I decided, as he was already turning and heading back out into the corridor. I quickly followed him, opting for grabbing my satchel, rather than spending time finding my key and locking the door. There was nothing in there worth pinching currently, after all. 'What's happened?' I asked. I was having to jog intermittently to keep up with him as we headed off down the corridor, and not just because I was five foot nothing to his six foot two. He was the sort of man who was born to lead and a great asset to the school, and with his brisk manner and his 'everything must be done yesterday' attitude, he was hard to keep up with at the best of times. But he was well liked by both the staff and the students, because he was down to earth, fair to a fault and enjoyed a laugh with the children, attributes that made for the best kind of teacher – well, in my humble opinion, anyway.

'Year eight assembly,' he said, directing his words half over his shoulder. 'Some sort of incident going on involving two of the pupils. I was told I was needed and so were you –' He turned and smiled a grim smile. 'And as you were on the way, I thought I'd scoop you up *en route*.'

So he was on his way *to* it. Which meant he must have been sent for or paged. 'A fight?' I asked.

'I believe so. Though I'm not yet quite sure … Ah –'

He didn't need to finish whatever it was he was about to say as we could hear the commotion before we saw it; well, the tell-tale sound of massed kids who, as our eyes soon confirmed, were all being herded out of the hall, most of them over-excited, chatting nine to the dozen about something exciting that had obviously gone down – and which probably livened up their morning no end.

'Settle down,' Donald barked, to no one in particular. He didn't need to – just his presence in the area was enough. The various form teachers were busy trying to wrestle back some order too, but the decibel levels suggested that whatever had happened was something more serious than just some radiator-related unrest.

That too was soon confirmed, as Andrea Halstead, one of the year eight form tutors, emerged from the hall and beckoned us to both follow her in.

'Oh, Mr Brabbiner,' she said, sounding as if she was still getting her breath back. 'Casey, hi. Bit of a to-do, I'm afraid. Might have been something and nothing, but Thomas over there's hit his head and Mr Reynolds and I were thinking that someone will probably need to take him down to A and E.'

'A and E?' Donald went straight into accident mode. 'What sort of head wound? Any bleeding? Did he pass out at any point?'

I looked across to where a group of assorted teachers, teaching assistants and one of the school secretaries, Janice Wells, were forming what looked like two separate human cordons around what must have been the two pupils in question, neither of whom I could properly see yet. What I could see, however, was a large muddle of chairs, several of them overturned, around which Barry, the caretaker, was methodically working, stacking the unaffected rows of chairs both in front of and behind the groups, and dragging them to their positions back against the walls. It was a circle of devastation that looked a little like something had been dropped in the middle of the hall from a great height. A fight, then, for definite.

Or perhaps not. 'I'm not sure,' Andrea said, 'We don't think so. But it's been bleeding rather copiously. It's up in his hair at the back –' she gestured to her own head to illustrate. 'Just above the back of his neck. Quite a nasty gash.'

'Wouldn't an ambulance be simpler?' Donald asked.

'We weren't sure,' Andrea said. 'I was going to call one, but then Janice reminded me about the roadworks on the way to the General. We were wondering if it wouldn't be easier for someone just to take him in their car. Mr Reynolds seems to have got the bleeding under control.'

'You want me to take him down in my car?' I asked. 'Who is it, anyway?'

'Lad called Thomas Robinson,' Andrea said. 'You probably haven't come across him – he's only been at the school for a couple of weeks or so, bless him. But, no, we were hoping you'd be able to take charge of Kiara, there. She's in no fit state to go back to her friends.'

She nodded towards the second of the two huddles, at the centre of which I could just make out a second pupil, who I now realised wasn't the gender I expected. 'Kiara?' I said. 'So it's a *girl*?'

Andrea nodded while Donald strode off to take charge of the patient and decide how best to get him to A and E. 'Kiara Bentley,' she confirmed. 'Have you had any dealings with her?'

As if to underline that even if I hadn't I might well do very soon, the subject of our discussion then started shouting. Shouting quite loudly, in fact; and making a great deal of noise for what looked like quite a small amount of pupil.

'What happened?' I asked Andrea, at a loss to work it out. 'Did the pair of them have a punch-up in the middle of assembly?'

'Not quite a full-on fight,' she said. 'But it certainly got physical. I didn't have the best view because they were half-way along a row, quite a way behind me. By the time I got to it, it was hard to make out what was going on. And she's still in a right state about it, as you can see. Come on, let's go and see if we can calm things down a bit, shall we? Then we can all get back on with our days.' She gave me a wry grin as we walked across the hall. 'One of *those* days, eh? Still, at least it's stopped everyone whining about the radiators.'

* * *

I'd already been involved in quite a few fight situations in the course of my job, and some things were common to all of them. The adrenalin rush, the urgent need to lower the emotional temperature and stop fists flying around, and the equally important need to establish the facts.

In that regard, coming into this one after the event left me at something of a disadvantage. On the one hand was this beefy-looking, scruffy, long-haired lad, clutching what looked like a tea-towel to his head, his white(ish) school shirt liberally splattered with blood and with the unmistakable pallor of a child who was in shock. And on the other hand was what seemed like a slip of a girl who seemed to be alternately sobbing and raging at the huddle of staff who were trying to calm her down.

But there was no point in trying to establish quite what had happened, not till the lad had been taken off to have his wound looked at and not till the girl – Kiara Bentley, that was it – was on a more even keel.

'This is Mrs Watson,' Andrea said, as we joined the small group surrounding her. Toni, the teaching assistant who'd been sitting beside her, immediately jumped up. 'Here,' she said, gesturing towards the seat she'd vacated.

I would have sat on it, too, the better to communicate with the girl, had it not been for the fact that at that exact moment Donald was leading the boy and his retinue out of the hall, which meant walking past us.

'You're a fucking *dick*!' the girl screamed suddenly, leaping up from her own seat, and only being stopped from lashing out at the boy again by Andrea's swift arresting arm.

'Kiara!' she barked, blocking her route to him. 'Stop it!'

'You're a fucking *bastard*!' she screeched, ignoring Andrea completely. 'And I hope they shrivel up and fall off as well!'

Hope *what* fall off? I wondered as I helped Andrea gently restrain her. 'Come on, love,' I said. 'This isn't helping anything, is it? Come on, how about you come with me, eh? Then you can tell me all about it, and –'

She ignored me as well. 'I've got more balls than you'll ever have *anyway*!' she yelled, shouting loud enough to make my left ear hurt, as Donald, with a short barked instruction of 'Enough!' disappeared with Janice and Thomas through the double doors. The boy, whose arresting mop of shoulder-length hair was flopping over his face, obscuring it, was half-doubled over, I noticed, and clearly in pain. I didn't need to see his face. I could hear him.

The penny dropped. *Balls*. That was what the girl said, hadn't she? Ouch.

'Enough, now!' Andrea repeated as between us we managed to guide the girl back to the seat she'd been sitting on, though, rigid with fury, she refused to sit down.

'You get back,' Andrea said to the two young teaching assistants still remaining, then turned her attention back to Kiara. 'Now, are you going to go with Mrs Watson nicely, my love? I know you're upset, but nobody can help you when you're screaming and hollering like this, can they? Come on, try and calm yourself down, okay?'

With the boy gone, all the fight seemed to have gone out of the girl anyway. 'I *hate* him!' she said, but it was a last angry parry, before dissolving into the latest of what looked like a few bouts of tears; she was wearing mascara – well, had been. By now most of it was on her cheeks.

'Kiara?' I said, trying to get her to focus her attention on me. 'What a pretty name. So, come on, how about you come to my classroom with me? You need something to drink, and to calm yourself down. Sort yourself out, eh?'

Not that she had anything with which to do that as yet, and I suddenly remembered that while delving into my bag earlier, I'd seen a half packet of tissues. I rummaged around for it and passed it to her so she could wipe her eyes and blow her nose on something a little kinder than the wodge of rough paper towel someone had obviously run and got from the loos.

She mumbled a thank you, and abruptly sat down again. It was almost as if her legs had given way beneath her, and I wondered if she was actually starting to faint. She was certainly pale enough. I sat beside her. 'We'll be fine if you want to get off as well now,' I said to Andrea. 'I'll take Kiara down to my classroom,' I said, glancing up at the big wall clock. Almost 12.15. It wouldn't be long till the bell went for lunch and the crowd outside – now dispersed presumably – would all be thronging back again, on their way down to the adjacent dinner hall.

'Come on, Kiara,' I said firmly as she dabbed at her eyes. 'Let's get out of here as well, eh?'

She looked up at me as if only properly seeing me for the first time. 'I *hate* him, miss,' she said.

* * *

Kiara Bentley was a tiny thing, slight in every sense. Which was to say she was my height but there was almost nothing of her. She also looked young for a year eight – was almost doll-like, in fact, with a small oval face which was currently half hidden behind a mass of curly, chocolate-coloured hair. She looked so forlorn too, now the fight had gone out of her; like the proverbial rag doll that gets parked in the corner by a child who's gone off in search of more interesting things to play with – a look enhanced by the two flaming spots on her pale cheeks. But the doll-like impression was at odds with the look in her eyes; a strange knowing look, causing the phrase 'old head on young shoulders' to pop unbidden into my mind.

'Am I in trouble, miss?' was the next thing she said to me, a full minute or so since Andrea departed for her tutor room, and we'd left the caretaker to finish clearing the hall. Still, at least she'd come with me readily enough.

'That's not going to be easy for me to answer, sweetheart,' I told her. 'As I have absolutely no idea what you've done.'

I waited, to see if she'd start to tell me the story. In my experience, kids either maintained a sullen silence or it all came rushing out, in one long torrent of denials, accusations and bitter recriminations, from which you then had to winkle out the facts.

'I never hurt his head. That wasn't me,' she said firmly. 'If that's what you're thinking. Just so you know. It *wasn't*.'

'I wasn't thinking anything,' I said mildly as we reached the door to my classroom. I opened it and stood aside to let her in. 'I'm completely in the dark. So how about you put your bag down and grab a chair, while I grab you a glass of juice, and you tell me all about it. How about that?'

It seemed Kiara Bentley had no problem with that at all. She had fallen asleep in assembly, she told me. She hadn't meant to – how could she? She hadn't realised she'd been asleep till she woke up.

Which was logical. I agreed she had a point. And when she'd woken up, she went on, it was to find her head was in Thomas's lap and that everyone around her was sniggering at her. 'And he'd been saying things,' she said, her voice now beginning to wobble, 'and messing about with my hair, miss, and …'

Her hand went to her hair then and as it did so I noticed that close to her temple there was a bald patch about the size of a ten-pence piece. 'Doing what things?' I asked, trying to visualise the scenario, all too aware that not all modern 12-year-olds were the sexual innocents their pre-teen status might suggest. Particularly groups of boys in close proximity to one another; it was a myth that it was only girls who got attacks of the giggles whenever it came to matters of sex. But what about that bald patch? Had he been responsible for that?

'Doing what to your hair?' I asked her.

'I don't know, miss, but something. You know. Messing about. Putting his hands in it. Pretending that I was giving him a, you know, a blow-job or something.'

Though it was slightly startling to hear such a phrase coming from what superficially seemed such a young innocent's mouth, this I could visualise all too easily, sadly. The sort of pubescent nonsense that young boys got up to everywhere. But one thing struck me. That must have been some nap she was having, for her to fall asleep so completely that him doing something like that didn't wake her up. That *was* odd. But then, I reasoned, he'd have had to be pretty quiet about his silliness, given that they were slap-bang in the middle of an assembly.

'And then you woke up,' I prompted, still wondering about the head wound and the hair and the hapless lad's testicles.

Kiara took a gulp of the orange juice I'd now poured for her before nodding. 'And I realised where I was and what was happening, and they were all saying stuff, like "Ooh, can I have a go next, Kiara?" Stuff like that. And he was, like, "Thanks for that. You're *really* good," and laughing at me and making faces and being an absolute *dick*.' Her eyes narrowed, her tears forgotten. 'So I got him back. Where it *hurts*.'

Which still didn't explain what happened next and I said so. Upon which Kiara explained, with a definite edge of pride, that she'd grabbed his balls so tightly that he'd actually screamed. 'Right in the middle of everything,' she said, the memory obviously firing her up all over again, 'because I did it just like my mum showed me. And he jumped up then, but I hung on and he kind of fell backwards and then – well, I don't know, really, because I'd let go by now and I didn't really see properly, but he was grabbing his balls and crying and then his chair tipped up somehow, and he fell back and then someone obviously stopped him, but then he slipped and – well, I don't know how really, but he, like, *proper* banged his head. On the edge of another chair I think it was. And that wasn't *anything* to do with *me*, miss. But then everyone started yelling and shouting and there was blood going everywhere, and then his mate Connor – *he's* a dick too – he went and grabbed me; grabbed my hair and started yelling in my face –'

'And pulled that clump out?'

'What?' She looked confused now. 'Oh, no,' she said, raising a hand to where I'd pointed then shaking her head. 'No, that wasn't him. That's nothing to do with it. Anyway, I told him I'd do the same to him as I'd done to his idiot friend and he let go. And then the teachers were all shouting and everyone round me's shouting at me too, saying *I* did it, but I *didn't* do it, miss. He fell over by himself. He banged his head by himself. Not that he didn't deserve it, miss. He's a *dick*.'

The lunch bell went then, as if to underline this assertion. And as it did so, I watched Kiara's hand go to the bald patch, seemingly unconsciously, and watched as she wound a single strand of hair around her finger and, with a sharp tug, plucked it out. I don't know why but something she'd said suddenly popped into my mind. *Just like my mum's showed me.* I filed the thought away.

'Doesn't that hurt you?' I asked.

'Doesn't what hurt?' she asked, her confusion at the question evident.

'When you pull out your hair like that,' I said. 'It must hurt when you do that, mustn't it?'

She looked down at her hand then let the hair go. She blushed. 'I know, miss,' she said. 'I really need to stop doing it, don't I?'

Kiara didn't go straight off to lunch. She didn't feel quite ready to face the world again yet, and I was happy to let her stay for a bit while I finished my coffee. She was on school dinners, and as there was always an enormous queue at the start of lunch-break, there was no particular urgency anyway

And now she'd got everything off her chest, she looked much brighter. 'Wow, this is cool, this place is, miss,' she observed, draining her juice. 'It's not at all like I thought it would be.'

'Oh, really?' I asked her, smiling. 'So you know all about my Unit, do you? So what *did* you think? What's the word on the street?'

'I dunno, miss,' she said, getting up and placing her cup back on my desk. 'Like a sort of cell or something – you know. Like a detention room. Not all nice and bright like this. It's lovely,' she added, surprising me with a smile that lit up her face. 'Really nice. What do you teach?'

'All sorts of things,' I told her. 'Though not the sort you might be thinking of. I'm not like the other teachers – we don't do the regular lessons in here.'

She walked across to the quiet corner. 'This is nice,' she said, peering round the side of the bookcases. 'Reminds me of being in the infants. You know? When you'd sit on bean bags for story time and stuff. And fall asleep halfway through,' she added, grinning across at me.

I laughed. 'And it's like that in here sometimes, as well. No one's ever too old to have a story read to them, are they? And yes, sometimes we do have the odd person nodding off. And we don't mind too much. As I say, this isn't like normal school.' Something occurred to me then. 'How about you this morning,' I asked her. 'You must have been out for the count and then some. Did you have a late night last night?'

I noticed her hand drift back to the same spot on her head again. It seemed to be entirely unconscious. 'Erm, a bit,' she admitted, but the pause before she answered was sufficient to spark a thought in me that there was possibly more to know. 'So how do you, like, end up here?' she added. 'I mean not *you*, miss. I mean the kids who get sent here. Why'd they come to you?'

I explained what the Unit was all about as I rinsed out my mug. How we took in the kids who were having problems of one kind or another and tried to help them rally their emotional forces and change some of the choices they made. 'So really,' I finished, 'it's a bit like a port in a storm. Because it can feel pretty stormy out there for some kids at some times. Well, a bit like it must have felt for you earlier on. Not to mention poor Thomas,' I added. 'He's had a bit of a time of it as well, hasn't he? Not that he didn't deserve you being furious with him,' I added. 'But it's a shame that he got hurt. Let's hope he's okay, eh?'

No pause this time. 'He's still a di – sorry, idiot. Sorry miss, but he *is*,' she added firmly. 'You should have *him* in here. He's *definitely* a problem kid.'

25

I couldn't help but smile at this. 'Well, he certainly has a problem today, doesn't he? But you know, Kiara, there's something you might not have thought about when it comes to "problem" kids – you know, the ones who are always naughty. They're almost always the ones that *have* the problems. That's what *makes* them naughty. And it's my job, once they're with me, to try and work it all out – unravel it so we can see everything more clearly, if you like.'

Kiara's hand drifted to her head again and, before I could distract her, she had wrapped her finger around another hair and tugged it out at the root. And as she absorbed what I'd said, I began to wonder. I wasn't sure why but there was something tugging at me too; some instinct that as yet had no real shape to it, but was persistently knocking on the door of my brain. The hair pulling was obviously a well-established tic, and a tic was a mechanism for self-soothing. And a need to self-sooth was generally a response to stress. And for an apparently fit young girl to fall fast asleep mid-morning … I didn't know what it added up to, but it did amount to something, as did what she said next.

'Can anyone come here, miss?' she said. 'You know, if they ask to?'

'That's not quite how it works,' I said. 'It's generally the teachers who decide. But to some extent, I suppose, yes. If a pupil obviously isn't managing in normal classes, then, as I was just saying, they can come here for a bit …'

'Like if they're too tired to do lessons?'

She looked directly at me, and again I got a glimpse of that rather 'knowing' look she had, and it made me suddenly wonder if I was being played here. It wasn't unheard of for a child to pretend they had problems just to escape the routine, or to have a regular pass out of some subject or class or teacher they didn't like. I'd been there before – as had Kelly, as had my alter ego, the other behaviour manager, Jim Dawson; having boys and girls practically begging for counselling, floods of tears, the whole kit and caboodle, only to find out later that they weren't distressed at all – had just forgotten their homework, or their football boots or netball kit or something and didn't dare turn up to class without it.

But, for all that Kiara seemed perfectly fine now, my antennae were quivering and, me being me, I needed to know why.

'I tell you what, sweetie,' I told her. 'Why don't you go off and get your lunch now. And while you're doing that, I'll have a word with your form teacher. You're still looking a bit pale to me, and I think you're still tired, aren't you? So, if you want to, how about I ask if you can come back here to me this afternoon? I've got new children coming in tomorrow and I need it prettying up a bit. How's that sound? Would you like to do that?'

'Could I?' This development seemed to please Kiara enormously. She reached for her backpack, which was bright pink and enormous, stuffed to bursting with goodness knows what. She'd be pretty exhausted just carrying that around all day, I mused.

'Yes, you could,' I said, nodding. 'Just go back to your tutor group for afternoon registration when the bell goes as normal, and then, all being well, she can send you straight back here.'

It was like magic. She fairly skipped out of the room.

I waited for a few seconds after Kiara left, then reached for my log book, so I could quickly scribble down the events of the past quarter of an hour, as well as get down the details of her version of events. It was such an automatic thing for me these days that I did it almost on auto-pilot. It was a vital part of my job and I was meticulous about it, too, because one thing I'd learned early on was that no matter how insignificant-seeming they might be at the time, the most mundane of facts, in conjunction with any timings, could end up being key ones at some point down the line. And though I obviously drew the line at writing 'very curiously knowing eyes' I still filed it in my brain, before grabbing my bag again and going in search of lunch and information. I had an itch now, and I was very keen to scratch it.

Chapter 3

Knowing that, in all likelihood, I wouldn't now get the chance to have lunch in the dining hall, I nipped into the staff-room to grab a sandwich from the new vending machine, and of course another coffee to warm me up. It was safe to say that the heating, or lack of it, was the hot topic of conversation, even if the grumbles and complaints were all about the cold. After waiting for a minute or so for the corridors to clear of the last remaining children making their way outside, I went along to the learning support department to see Julia Styles.

'Ah, Casey,' she said, smiling as I entered her office, 'I thought you might be popping in. I guess you want to know a little bit more about your new students. Grab a chair and I'll see what I can find. Not that I'm any wiser than you are at the moment, to be honest. Don't even know who they are. What with the blasted radiators and everything, I've not even had a chance to look myself yet.'

'Well, yes, that would be helpful,' I said, sitting down on the chair to the left of her desk, 'but no rush. Actually I'm here about a year eight girl. Kiara Bentley? I just picked her up from the assembly hall after that fracas earlier. You know about that?'

Julia nodded. 'I do. Don stopped by before he left and filled me in.'

'He took the boy himself then?'

Julia nodded. 'And fingers crossed all is well. Though the consensus seemed to be that he was a great deal more fixated on – ahem – another part of his anatomy.'

I smiled. 'I'm not surprised.' I told her the version of events Kiara had outlined to me – a version I didn't doubt was pretty accurate, too.

She rolled her eyes. 'So he's had something of an education today, by the sound of it. And how's Kiara? She okay now? Don said she was in a right state.'

'She's okay now. I've just left her. She's taken herself off to lunch. But I'm going to track down her form teacher and see if she can come back to me this afternoon. There's something about her ... I don't know, Julia. It might be something or nothing, but she's clearly over-tired, and she's got this hair-pulling thing going on. You know what I'm like,' I added, seeing the grin spreading on my colleague's face. 'Just a bit of an itch I've got.'

'We-ell,' she said, 'funnily enough, there *is* something on Kiara Bentley's record, so that itch of yours certainly isn't way off-beam. It's historic, though, so don't get too excited. An incident from back at the start of year seven. Hang on,' she said, rising from her chair, 'I'll pull her file out.'

It didn't take Julia long to find the file, and to explain that not long after Kiara had joined the school, another year seven pupil had reported that she'd had cuts up her arm – cuts that, when questioned by the child, Kiara had freely admitted she'd done herself. When confronted by her teacher, Kiara had been equally upfront, brushing it off as silliness; saying that she'd read a magazine article about self-harming and, stupidly – her admission – had decided to try it herself, just to find out 'if it hurt'.

Which naturally got my itch going all the more. 'She was apparently quite matter-of-fact,' Julia said. 'I remember talking to the teacher myself. Said she had absolutely no intention of doing anything so silly ever again. Though, naturally, not entirely convinced, we brought the mum in for a chat. And she was extremely upset about it all, as you can imagine, but could offer nothing in the way of an explanation for it. Had no idea what had possessed her, apparently. Her inclination was to put it down to attention seeking, and we were inclined to agree with her. She did say she'd been working long hours – perhaps too long – and, well, we all know what it's like for some of our working single parents, don't we? And I don't think there's much in the way of extended family to provide support. Anyway, Kiara was offered counselling, obviously, but she point-blank refused, after which there was little we could do about it other than try and keep an eye on her.'

'So it was left at that point?' I asked. 'No one continued to monitor her?'

Almost as soon as the words were out I felt myself redden, realising how incredulous my tone had been. I saw something flash across Julia's face too, perhaps unsurprisingly, as if she couldn't quite believe I might be daring to insinuate that she'd not done her job probably.

But it soon disappeared; I think she realised I really wasn't pointing fingers. She had had a big, busy department to run, and she ran it brilliantly. And she couldn't possibly be expected to have eyes and ears everywhere, any more than the rest of us could.

Even so, stated so baldly, it did seem surprising that something so potentially serious could have been dropped so quickly. No, I wasn't backing down in that regard. And the itch was itching fiercely.

'Well, of course we did what we could for a while,' Julia assured me. 'Kept our eyes open; informed the obvious teachers in the PE and Drama departments to be on the look-out for cuts and scratches on her arms and legs and so on. But other than that, our hands were – and *are* – a bit tied.' Julia spread her palms then. 'And, well, since then, there's been nothing to ring alarm bells. Yes, she's a bit of a loner. Not a garrulous child. Keeps herself to herself. But this was back at the start of year seven and we're now more than halfway through year eight, and, as I say, no one's flagged up any cause for concern more recently.'

Yet, I thought. *Yet*. And I begged to differ. 'I think there might be now,' I said, hoping I didn't sound as if I knew better, but at the same time aware that it needed to be said. 'I think she's still self-harming, just a lot more discreetly.'

'Really?' asked Julia, leaning forward in her seat, if not exactly pricking up her ears. It was always a delicate balancing act, trying to observe the protocols of position and seniority; it wasn't up to me to try and tell her her job. 'And what makes you think that, Casey?'

'Not cutting,' I quickly clarified. 'Nothing like that. But she *has* got a bald patch on her head – quite a big one – and I watched her myself as she was pulling her own hair out; she's not even really aware that she's doing it. I know that in itself doesn't scream self-harm – it's more like a tic – but given what you've just told me about her history of self-harming, I'm even more inclined to think than I was when I got in here that there's some underlying problem still present. And she's clearly come into school exhausted this morning.'

Julia picked up a pen and clicked the end a couple of times as she thought; a little tic of her own. Then she nodded. 'I take your point. We certainly shouldn't ignore it. And you never know, if you have a couple of hours with her, you might get her to open up – sniff out whatever's to be sniffed out in your usual Sherlocky style. But what about the other kids you've got coming tomorrow? Shall we run through them quickly now together?'

I shook my head. 'Don't worry now,' I said. 'Perhaps you can spare me ten minutes at the end of the day instead? Or first thing tomorrow?'

Like me, Julia was invariably in early. In a job that often meant being reactive once the children were put into the equation, there was a lot to be said for having 30 or so precious minutes at either end of the day in which you could be proactive instead, not to mention time to organise your thoughts. 'Of course,' she said. 'Just come and find me – I'll be here. And right now, you need to get that sandwich down you, don't you? Mind you, a hot toddy would be preferable today, wouldn't it? Honestly, Casey. It's not on, this, is it? I mean, it's not as if it's –'

'Rocket science?' I supplied for her, grinning.

I checked my watch as I hurried back to the staff-room. We had a bank of computers there, in the quiet room that was just off the main communal area, and if there was one free, I probably had just enough time to log in before the bell went, and do a bit of speed-research as I ate.

And I was in luck. I was able to get onto one right away.

I never failed to be awed by the usefulness of the internet. Luddite that I was (most new technology tended to baffle me initially) I had come to really embrace the amazing free resource that was the plethora of information on the web. What would probably be taken for granted in no time at all was, at that time (for me, at any rate), an incredibly helpful tool. You had to be savvy about it, of course – there was probably plenty of mis-information on there too – but much to my own children's consternation and horror, I'd enrolled in a course at our local library during the last holidays; a kind of idiot's guide or, as my son called it, 'idiot *old* person's guide' to the magic of the internet. He might have laughed – and he did, like all smart-alec computer-savvy kids – but I'd actually found it very useful. I'd learned a lot; in fact I now considered myself able enough to even keep tabs on what the young people who came to me got up to when I allowed them to work on my computer in school – a teaching skill of increasing importance.

Having opened my typically impenetrable plastic sandwich wrapper as quietly as I could (you weren't supposed to eat and drink near the computers) I typed 'pulling out hair, children' into the search engine. Up came the results, and the first was one long word: trichotillomania. Intrigued by the fancy name (I had to read it twice, slowly) I started to read.

What I learned immediately was that I was wrong to assume that Kiara's hair pulling was a sign of continuing self-harm; in terms of something or nothing, perhaps it *was* a 'nothing' then. Because according to everything I was reading, it had nothing whatsoever to do with wanting to hurt oneself, or indeed give oneself a bald patch. It was a neurological condition, more like a compulsion than a habit – indeed a tic – and once started was extremely difficult to stop. It was more common in girls, apparently, and the usual age for onset was around 11, though it could apparently start earlier than that.

What did stand out, though, was that hair pulling wasn't confined to any particular cultural or social group; even the happiest, most settled children could develop the compulsion, just as easily as an unhappy or abused child could. But as I'd suspected, it *was* a reaction to stress, and since that bald patch had clearly been there for a while, it was a stress that was ongoing.

So it was probably a case of finding out what form the stress took, and on that score I had little to go on. It might be something as straightforward as the start of puberty and anxiety about the changes that were going on inside Kiara; many girls developed issues with body-confidence around that time, and, physically, Kiara seemed quite a 'young' 12-year-old to me. It might be bullying – in which case, was it a response to the stress inherent in coming to school? Or was it home-based – something to do with her relationship with her mum? There could be so much going on that we didn't know about, after all.

But it was pointless to speculate. All I could do was watch and wait and wonder – and try to tune into what it might be that gave her that look – as if she had the weight of the world on those narrow shoulders. That and the evident fatigue. What was that about?

'Now that's a very serious Casey face,' came a voice from behind me. 'I can see it in the screen. You want a coffee before the off?'

I swivelled around on the swivel chair to find Kelly in the doorway, brandishing my mug. There was an encouraging tendril of steam coming from it, too.

'Just concentrating,' I told her, accepting it gratefully. 'Been trying to find out a bit about trichotillomania. Tricho – yes, I got that right. Trichotillomania. Did you hear about the hoo-hah in the year eight assembly?'

'Sure did,' Kelly said. 'All poor Donald needed.'

'Well, the girl, Kiara Bentley – I took her back to the Unit with me. Hence the search. She's got quite some bald patch in her hair. And the whole business – I mean, just how tired d'you have to be to end up with your head in a boy's lap?'

'Assuming that *was* the case. He'll probably say differently.'

I shook my head. 'He might well, but I'm pretty sure I believe her.'

'And you know what?' Kelly said, pointing a finger towards the screen. 'That does figure. *Yes.* It really does. One of the Maths teachers – whatshisface – was talking about Kiara the other day – yes, I'm *sure* he said the name Kiara – and saying that she kept falling asleep in lessons. Yes, I'm sure it was her. I'll double check.'

'Would you? And if you run into anyone else who might have dealings with her, ask them about her as well. I just have this sense that there's more to this whole thing than meets the eye. Anyway, she's coming back to me after lunch. Maybe I'll get something more out of her then.'

'And some cheap labour too,' Kelly said, winking. 'Nice work, Dr Watson!'

Kiara was already outside my door when I returned after the lunch break, having let her form teacher know she'd be with me for the rest of the day. Once again, I was struck by how doll-like she looked, from her petite, elfin face, to her nicely pressed school uniform, which looked as if it had only recently been bought. Now she was composed again, she positively gleamed with grooming, and I mused that if the school had to select a poster girl to reflect their sartorial benchmark, then this little girl would be she.

'Ready to roll your sleeves up?' I asked her, as I unlocked the door and opened it. 'What are you getting out of this afternoon anyway?'

'Double English,' she said, without hesitation.

'Well, we'll be doing double decorating instead,' I said. 'That okay with you?'

'That's fine, miss,' she said, taking the pink backpack from her shoulders and parking it on a nearby chair. 'I'm good at decorating. I painted a whole bedroom wall last weekend, all by myself. Pink,' she added, grinning.

I smiled at her. 'How did I know you were going to say that? So, what would you like to do, sweetie? My walls all look bare, the glass in my door looks boring, and all my plants need a watering and a talking-to, so – take your pick. What are you best at?'

She chose to create some artwork for the door, which suited me fine. Doing something physical was often key to getting kids to open up. Rather than sit them down and start interrogating them, I'd learned over the years that a softly-softly, lateral approach was usually better – get them doing something alongside you that kept half their minds occupied, and a child would often relax enough to open up a little.

I was quite the expert at it, in fact. With my son Kieron, who had a mild form of autism called Asperger's Syndrome (as it was known back then, anyway), I had become well practised in winkling out the nuts and bolts of anxiety in a child who preferred to bottle everything up. If he was struggling with something, I'd nag him to help me with something in the house or garden and then, once he was 'in the zone' of whatever he was doing, he'd be so much more receptive to sharing what was on his mind and we'd be able to find a solution together. It was never *quite* as simple as that with the kids in school, obviously, because we didn't have that history and mother/son bond. But, eventually, after building up that all-important trust, they usually did start to talk.

And hopefully Kiara would, too. 'Right then,' I said as I clapped my hands together. 'The door it is. I'll leave the design ideas to you.'

Kiara threw herself into the work with gusto. Within ten minutes, she was carefully cutting out the giant cardboard Easter egg shapes she had decided would be perfect. She'd made four of them in total, having checked with me first, one for her to write her name on – 'Kiara woz 'ere!' she joked – and one for each of the three children who I told her would be joining me in the morning. She was using different coloured card for each and decorating them with contrasting borders. 'You can explain to them that they have to write their names across this middle bit,' she said. 'And then they can stick them to the glass in the door. That should brighten the place up a bit, miss, shouldn't it?'

A girl after my own heart, I thought, as I remembered the flowers that had previously adorned the door, all decorated by my last brood of children. I also noted that she seemed both alert and engaged and, with her hands fully occupied, was refraining from absent-mindedly fiddling with her hair.

'That's a great idea,' I agreed, having a bit of a re-think, 'and since you're so good with the art stuff, you can put up some new borders round my display panels, while I get on with sorting out the books.'

'I've always been good at practical things,' she said. 'I get it from my mum. That's what she always says – that we're both really good with our hands. But I'll help you sort the books out as well, once I'm done. I'm good at that too.'

But it turned out there was something Kiara Bentley was even better at. The decorations made, she did indeed join me in the quiet corner and between us we pulled out every single book in there, dusted them off, categorised them and put them all back in their new positions, after which I left her to it, putting labels on the front of the shelves so everyone who borrowed a book would know where to put it back, while I had a quick clear-out of my desk.

I hadn't gleaned a great deal, only snippets of rather bland info; that this slight and pretty 12-year-old liked pink, enjoyed pop magazines and wearing make-up, that her mum didn't like her dad so they got divorced when she was little, and that, mostly, she didn't really have friends round the house because her mum didn't like the place being messed up when she was out at work. There was nothing much, all told, to inflame the itch further, and perhaps, despite the hair-pulling, there wouldn't be. Perhaps she was just a lonely-ish kind of kid, living a less than perfect childhood, with a mum who worked long hours, and who wasn't getting enough sleep; she wouldn't have been the first and she wouldn't be the last, after all.

I'd try to keep an eye on her, as far as I could, and I *had* shared my concerns. But I knew that, come tomorrow, I'd have three new demanding charges, all with problems needing interventions that would probably fill both my time and my head. 'You want another orange juice, love?' I asked her as I flicked the switch on the kettle. And when she didn't answer, I immediately went over to the quiet corner, already knowing what I would probably find there.

And I did. I put my head round the bookcases to find her curled up on a bean bag, fast asleep again and gently snoring. I stepped away again, made my coffee, finished clearing my desk, and only when it got to five minutes before the bell was due to buzz for home time did I return to the quiet corner and shake her gently awake.

She woke up wide-eyed, disorientated, blinking.

I smiled, hands on hips, as she rubbed her eyes and stood up. 'You are definitely burning too much midnight oil, young lady,' I told her. 'Early night for you tonight and that's an order.'

'I'm sorry,' she said. 'I just sat down to do the labels on the bottom shelf and … well,' she added sheepishly, 'I must have drifted off.'

'Tell me, Kiara,' I said, driven by a sudden and very powerful instinct, 'would you like to come back here tomorrow?'

It would prove to be the best instinct I'd had in a long time. A life-saver, almost. A childhood-saver, definitely.

'Yes, please,' she said. And thank God she did.

Chapter 4

I slammed the car door with my usual gusto as I got out of it on our drive. Not because I wanted to make any sort of statement, but because it was the only way to be sure of it actually shutting. My poor little Fiesta was 12 years old now, but despite its little 'idiosyncrasies' (well, that was how I liked to think of them) I was still resistant to Mike's endless tutting and head-shaking, and banging on about how I should really look for something newer.

The noise brought Kieron to the door anyway. 'Ah, Mum,' he said, looking shifty, 'just so you know, we got a half day today so I've brought Si home to work with me on some music. Which is important. Because it's stuff we're doing for college. So I don't suppose you would put on some earmuffs or something, would you?'

'*Earmuffs*?' I asked him.

'Yeah,' he said, looking at me as if I was ridiculously slow on the uptake. 'You know, so you can't, like, *hear* us?'

Lovely, I thought, wondering quite why Kieron thought I'd be able to whip up a pair of earmuffs out of nothing. As far as I could remember, I had never owned a pair of earmuffs in my life – a lack that wasn't lost on me given that I'd spent most of the day lightly chilled, like the ready-meals in the local branch of Tesco.

'It's that bad, is it?' I asked him, dropping my satchel onto the hall floor for the moment, to sit among the small gathering of abandoned trainers. It was certainly odds-on that it might be. Kieron was taking a media studies course at college and had recently developed an obsession with 'mixing beats', whatever that was. All I knew was that it had involved Mike spending a ridiculous amount of money on some turntables and a mixing desk, and then lots of noise. That was definitely the only word to describe what was floating down the stairs to me right now. Well, to be fair, that one word was a bit of a generalisation. 'Strangled cat mixed with several hundred fingers being scraped down a blackboard all at once' was quite a good description too.

Si, aka Simon, was on the same course. He and Kieron had been friends since they'd both started high school, so I'd known him for years, but now I saw rather more of him than I ever did before; amazing how a pair of turntables (wash my mouth out – I must remember that they are 'decks') could totally take over a pair of teenage boys' lives. Not to mention turning me into my mother. Much as I was horrified to realise it was happening, my new catch phrase seemed to be 'Turn that down!'

I bit my lip to stop myself from saying it this time. 'Not a chance, kiddo,' I said instead as I slipped off my jacket. 'Tell you what – how about you and Si put on your headphones and listen to your "tunes" through those. How's that for an idea? I need to get dinner ready, don't I?'

'Mother,' Keiron said, shaking his head in disdain. 'You are so *old* school! *Fine*, then,' he added, in a voice heavy with resignation. 'We'll try to be quiet, then.' He then turned tail and began heading back up the stairs. But not before adding that, where dinner was concerned, just pizza for him and Si would be fine. 'Upstairs, yeah? So we can crack on with our work,' he explained, without so much as the tiniest pinch of irony.

What was it they said was a great leveller? Time? Death? Education? I wasn't sure, but as I hung my jacket over the newel post, I decided 'going home' was probably right up there in the top ten of things that kept your feet on the ground, if not your chakras re-aligned. Evidence of recent occupation was strewn around my living room, where some living had evidently been done. My perfectly placed scatter cushions were now strewn across the sofa any old how, the TV, though muted, was playing some music station and as I looked through to my kitchen and dining area, I could see that I had the joy of a sink full of washing up that hadn't been there when I'd left it.

What planet had I been on when I looked forward to the time when my kids were older, confident that the working day might just mean exactly that? That I wouldn't then have to come home and start work all over again? As yet, there'd not only been no sign of that happening – it seemed to be getting even worse. Because not only was I expected to feed my own husband and offspring – these days there was more often than not someone else wanting feeding; or who just happened to be around when it was dinner time.

As a family, we'd swelled our ranks as well. Our daughter Riley was now going steady with her boyfriend David, so much so that they were currently saving up to buy a house. Which was wonderful, because he was a lovely lad, and a great foil for our feisty daughter, but with every bit of spare cash being directed towards their savings, their days of living the high life, gadding about, going out and eating in restaurants had been replaced with the more cost-effective and time-honoured tradition of either eating at our house or his parents'.

I didn't mind all the extra work this entailed. I really didn't. Well, I didn't mind 99 per cent of the time, anyway; it didn't go down well with my more rigorously twenty-first-century dwelling colleagues but I loved looking after my little family. But every day, for about five minutes, when I was feeling that enervating just-home-from-work tiredness, I wished I didn't get home before Mike and Riley, so that it could be *me* walking in to the smell of something nice cooking, rather than them.

Sadly, I had no access to that universe currently, and as I wouldn't be letting Kieron loose in the kitchen any time soon (pizza was nice, but not every day for all eternity) I rolled up my sleeves up and cracked on. And as I did so, I wondered about Kiara and what sort of home she'd be returning to tonight. I couldn't seem to help it. I had so little to go on, and what I had was hardly earth-shattering, but there was something about that girl that had really got under my skin.

I'd not had a chance to catch up with Julia Styles after school the previous day so the following morning I set my alarm early and, having remembered to take a cardigan in case the radiators were still iffy, the first thing I did when I got into work was to pay her a visit.

'You'll never guess what,' she said, almost the second I stepped into her office.

I grinned. 'Try me. Erm … no, hang on. Let me see. They've decided to cancel the inspection because they already know how brilliant we are.'

She shook her head. 'You wish. No, Thomas Robinson.'

'Thomas who?' I said.

'Doesn't ring a bell?'

'No, it doesn't,' I admitted. 'No, wait. Hang on. Maybe it does. It's definitely ringing something.' I made a show of tipping my head from side to side to check.

'It should do,' Julia said, beckoning to the chair beside her desk. 'He's the lad who banged his head in the hall yesterday after that to-do with Kiara Bentley.'

'Of *course*,' I said, the penny dropping. 'How's he doing?'

'Fine, by all accounts,' she said. She pulled a file towards her as I sat down. 'Apparently looked much worse than it was – often the case with heads, isn't it? Bleed like the devil. They steri-stripped it apparently. No concussion or anything. So that's good.' She smiled. 'Though not from Donald's point of view. Three hours he was down there –

the mum couldn't be found, apparently, and there was no alternative contact in his file. He's a new lad,' she added, by way of explanation. 'Only been here a fortnight or so, bless him. Something of a baptism of fire!'

Certainly something of a reminder that silly, lewd behaviour was not the way to win friends and influence people – particularly girls. Though it was obviously good to know the wound was only minor. 'Anyway, what about him?' I asked, remembering Julia's opening comment.

'This'll make you smile,' she said. 'He's one of the lads you're down to have joining the Unit. I only just realised. Only part time for the moment. To see how it goes. According to what Donald put here, he needs a bit of "socialising".'

I smiled. Socialising could encompass all sorts of things, though from the evidence of the previous days it sounded fairly cut and dried; he needed to learn how to behave himself. He'd gone slightly feral, his file said, the family having been steadily making their way north from London over the last couple of months, staying with friends and relatives and moving around a lot, in order to escape the abusive ex who was apparently still trying to track them down.

For Thomas and his four older sisters this had meant nothing in the way of schooling, and having spent so much time away from structure and routine, he was badly in need of some boundaries and order in his life.

'He's been marked out as being a little "wild",' Julia clarified, 'as you'll have already noticed yourself. Wild and a little bit too streetwise for his age.'

'Not to mention keen to make his mark,' I said, remembering what Kiara had told me. Because I didn't doubt all his nonsense had been much more about impressing his new friends than real sexual intention.

'You said it,' Julia agreed. 'And now, given their confrontation yesterday, I'm wondering if we should have a bit of a rethink. He was only due to be with you for half the week in any case, but perhaps we should hold off? Kelly tells me you've suggested Kiara stay with you for a few days. Is that right?'

I nodded. 'Yes, that's one of the things I wanted to talk to you about. I just feel there's more to know, and, since she seems happy to spend a little time with me – well, you know me. I'm determined to find out what it is. You know, something else occurred to me last night as well. She really *is* a loner, isn't she? I was just wondering why she'd have been sitting with that group of boys in the first place. Where were her girlfriends? Does she even *have* a regular group of friends? A lot of her stress might be because she's feeling isolated, mightn't it?'

'Like I said, she's always been a quiet one,' Julia said. 'Doesn't mix much at all. And that's fine, Casey. Of course it is. I trust your instincts totally. And it's not like you're over-run right now. But I'm not sure throwing those two together is going to be a terrifically good idea, are you? I mean, I know they're in the same tutor group anyway so they'll be back together for registration and so on in the fullness of time, but in the short term it's hardly going to make for harmony in the classroom, is it?'

'No,' I said, 'Probably not. But it's a bridge we can cross when we get to it, isn't it? Once he's back in school.'

'He already is,' she said. 'I saw him arriving earlier. He's sitting in your very own breakfast club even as we speak, no doubt. Can't seem to keep him away!'

Setting up the breakfast club had been one of the first initiatives I'd thrown myself into when I joined the school. It tended to be a mixture of the proverbial 'latchkey kids' and those whose parents left for work too early to get them up for school and make breakfast; some of these kids could just as easily get ready and eat breakfast at home but would rather have the company of friends than be alone in an empty house. I completely got that, and whatever the reasons for them attending, it made me happy to know that at least these kids could start the day after a feast of a meal. This was all thanks to the rather generous budget we had been allocated, as often was the case with new initiatives. It enabled us to provide the kids with cereals, fruit, juices, toast, peanut butter, etc. for a nourishing and balanced breakfast.

'*Really*?' I said to Julia now. 'He's already back? Wouldn't the hospital have advised him to stay at home and rest for a few days?'

Julia shrugged. 'They could well have. But it clearly hasn't happened, has it? I think his mum has some sort of temporary job, which means Thomas goes to school. As far as I know, they don't have anyone local who can support them as yet. My guess is that as he's been given a clean bill of health down in A and E, it's more a case of "go in and if you feel ill tell a teacher" than "stay home with me and I'll mop your fevered brow", don't you?'

I agreed she was probably right. 'But I'm happy to take him in anyway. No time like the present for the two of them to patch things up, is there? As I say, they'll both be back in the same tutor group before you know it, after all. And you know me – I'll find a way to use it to my advantage. Sex ed. Being kind. Name calling and so on. No, it's fine. So who else do I have as well?'

Julia quickly ran through the other names and a little bit about them. The girl, Chloe, did turn out to be the one Kelly had told me about, and the other boy was a year seven lad called Jonathan, who had been living with a foster family for the past six months. He was apparently angry and disruptive and on a behaviour-modification programme with his foster mum; having to earn 'mummy dollars' for good behaviour, in order to have currency to spend on treats, such as TV and computer time, and having friends round.

His was a sad case; abandoned by his mother when he was just a toddler, Jonathan had been left in the care of a father who had significant learning difficulties. He'd entered the care system, aged 11, when a neighbour had found him scavenging in their dustbin in search of food.

'This one apparently needs a bit of socialising too, Casey,' Julia told me. 'Looks young for his age – a bit like butter wouldn't melt – but has a very world-weary, angry, unhappy head on his shoulders; the consensus seems to be that, despite the great work his foster mum's doing with him, his behaviour is steadily getting worse. You're going to have your hands full with him, by all accounts.'

I was going to have my hands full, period, I reckoned. But that was fine. That was just the way I liked it.

The next thing I had to do was telephone Kiara's mother and let her know her daughter would be spending a few days with me. This was standard practice: it was obviously important to keep parents in the loop and, hopefully, to keep them on side. It wasn't always possible, because some kids came from difficult, complex backgrounds, but where there was a parent or guardian at home who wanted the best for their child, then it made sense for us to work as a team. And most of the time that was what we achieved. Initial reactions could be varied, however. Some parents were grateful for the extra support, but some were not; either suspicious of our motives, or concerned about their child being labelled, or just plain defensive about the whole thing, and angry that we were trying to 'interfere'.

I wasn't sure whether Kiara would have mentioned the incident the previous day or not, but I decided it was worth mentioning it to her mother, if only because her response might give me a further insight into how things were at home, and perhaps shed light on Kiara's evident fatigue. This would also provide the reason given for having her with me; not much in itself but, along with the hair-pulling habit, it was reason enough, and I hoped I'd be able to get her on side.

Before I made the call, however, I would need to clear it with Gary Clark. After grabbing my second caffeine fix of the day, and armed with the usual wodge of mail and memos from my pigeonhole, I set off down the unusually quiet staff corridor to his office, only passing Barry, the caretaker, and a heating engineer. I smiled as I saw the new sign on Gary's door. It was a smart black placard, embossed in gold with the words *Child Protection Officer*, and he was as proud of it as he might have been to have a star on Hollywood Boulevard. In a school, the little things were sometimes the big things.

'Very official,' I said, grinning as I opened the door and nodded to it. 'Do I need to start calling you sir or something now?'

'Lord Clark will do just fine, Casey,' Gary said, laughing as he pulled out a chair for me. 'And I see you've already got a coffee. At the very least, we should celebrate with a choccy biscuit, don't you think?'

I shook my head. 'You know what it's like with addictions, Gary. I try not to start too early in the day. I only need five minutes of your time this morning anyway. Just to let you know what I'm doing with Kiara Bentley.'

I quickly ran through my thoughts, and let him know I wanted to spend a little time working with her. 'So I was thinking I'd try to get hold of her mum this morning. Fill her in – assuming Kiara hasn't already told her, that is – and see if she can enlighten me at all.'

'That would be helpful, certainly,' Gary said. 'Though if memory serves, she wasn't particularly forthcoming last time. And she doesn't strike me as a terribly maternal mum. Still, it's obviously important to touch base with her. Let me know how it goes. Now, are you sure you won't be tempted by a chocolate biscuit?'

I fled the room before I caved in and changed my mind.

I went to my own room to make the call to Kiara's mother. The quiet area of the staff-room would do ordinarily, but at this time of day it was like Piccadilly Circus, filling up with teachers with their own busy agendas; last-minute calls to make, coffees to be gulped down, things to be photocopied, gossip to be shared. I was also keen to be 'in situ' when my new kids arrived, as it felt important to be there to welcome them and set them at their ease.

It's impossible to get much of a sense of a person via a phone call, but one thing was clear. She was prickly. 'She's on her *way*,' she snapped immediately when I told her who I was and where I was calling from, and didn't sound that convinced even when I explained that I wasn't calling to chastise her for sending Kiara in late, because I didn't even know she was going to be.

Though a glance at my watch confirmed that she would be. 'I run the behaviour unit,' I clarified. Which seemed to inflame Kiara's mother further.

'The what?' she wanted to know. 'Why does she have to go in there? There's nothing wrong with her behaviour. And if you're calling about that lad she gave what-for to, serve him bloody well right, as well. Little sh…' She stopped and regrouped. 'Little sod. And what about her exams and stuff? Won't it affect her school work if she's taken out of lessons?'

I assured Mrs Bentley that any important work would be sent through to me and that I would personally make sure it got done. I also explained that for a few days I'd be working closely with Kiara, getting to know her better and, in doing so, perhaps getting to the root of why she was so apparently tired and stressed in school.

'How is she at home?' I asked. 'I'm told there were similar concerns about her last year. How has she been at home? Does she seem stressed to you?'

'Not particularly,' she said. 'I mean, she's not the most relaxed of kids at the best of times, is she?' She sighed heavily. 'Look, the school already know the sort of hours I work. I do my best, alright? We're not all living in fairy land, you know. Life can be hard at times. That's how it works in the real world. I do my best, like I said.'

'I know, Mrs Bentley. I completely understand that. It must be hard, trying to make ends meet, have to be both mum and dad ...'

A humourless laugh crackled down the line. 'Oh, pur-*lease* don't get me started on *him*,' she said. 'That bloody waster. Turns up out of the blue like a bad penny, and it's all "daddy" this and "daddy" that. I don't know why she bothers with him, I really don't.'

'Her dad?' I asked, surprised. 'I hadn't realised he was still on the scene. So she still sees him then?'

'Is *back* on the scene. After being AWOL for eight years. She's seeing him most weekends. He's flavour of the month, he is, currently.' She sniffed. 'Look, it's not ideal, but it's not for me to stop her seeing him if she wants to, is it? And with me working nights at the care home twice a week, well, at least I know where she is, don't I? Idiot that he is. Stupid pillock treats her like a bloody five-year-old.'

I wasn't quite sure what to make of that but didn't know how to frame a question that would provide an answer. I left it.

'So this is through the courts, is it?' I said instead, remembering what Julia had said about their divorce having been acrimonious.

'Oh no,' she said, 'we didn't bother with any of that. He buggered off soon as, and good bloody riddance.'

'So there was no contact?'

'Not for a long time. Not since she was about five. He was just so bloody unreliable that in the end I stopped taking her; it was too upsetting for her. Not till he moved back to the area a couple of months back and wanted to know if he could start seeing her again. And, like I say, it's not for me to deprive her of her father, is it? Not now she's the age she is. Typical daughter. Dotes on him. Easy that, though, isn't it? *He's* not the one having to scrape together a living, is he? Or discipline her, or buy her uniform or make her tidy her room or any of that. So it's all "daddy" this and "daddy" that. Like he can do no bloody wrong ...'

I stepped in while she paused to gather breath.

'Well, that's all really useful information,' I said quickly. 'Perhaps it's the changes that have led to her feeling a little strung out.' Not to mention the obvious bad feeling between her parents, I thought, but didn't say. It was *so* obvious, too – kids were always badly affected by warring parents – but to say so to this woman I'd not yet even met would be to cross a line I didn't feel I should cross at this stage. I didn't have all the facts, after all.

But I was quite keen to add to the ones I already had. 'Which was why I thought it might be helpful,' I added, 'if I could chat to you together at some point as well.'

'What, drag me up to the school?' Mrs Bentley seemed affronted at the very thought.

'No, no – at home,' I explained. 'We tend to like to do that wherever possible. Feels less formal that way – all the better to help the child open up.'

All the better to get a different perspective on the relationship between child and carer as well. You could learn so much more when you saw a child on home turf.

'When would this be?' she wanted to know. 'I told you. I work long hours.'

'When it works best for *you*,' I reassured her. 'Whenever you feel you can fit it in. After school one day perhaps? Just for an hour or so. No more than that. How about I give you Gary Clark's number and you get in touch and let him know when will suit you best. You remember him, don't you?'

Mrs Bentley said she did, and promised she would call him when she could, and as I ended the call I pondered the reality of their domestic situation: the daily grind of working long hours, for meagre pay, in order to bring in sufficient money to keep a roof over her and her daughter's head. It *was* hard; for some families, it was nigh on impossible. She was right. This was the real world, not fairy land.

The poor kid, I thought, as I began preparing trays for my new charges. Stuck in the middle of adversarial parents and their rows wasn't a nice place to be. Nor was having to be up all hours and living a peripatetic life, without proper bedtimes, much less a mum there to kiss you goodnight and to wish you sweet dreams. It was no wonder she was tired and on edge.

It would certainly explain why she was coming to school tired, and why she'd developed the self-soothing habit of pulling out her hair. It would possibly also explain why she kept herself to herself. Yes, I thought, making a mental note to write up my conversation with Mrs Bentley, I probably had my answer right there.

Well, possibly.

Chapter 5

There was a knock on my classroom door a few minutes before the bell went, which I answered to find a trio of children standing outside. The first I recognised immediately as Thomas, the lad who'd had the head injury the previous morning. His hair was longer than I'd realised. Almost past his shoulders, it looked like it was crying out for a good brush, and though his uniform had clearly seen better days, it certainly hadn't seen a washing machine in a while. Neither, I judged – hazarding a guess – had the tattered but expensive-looking trainers that were on his feet but not the uniform list. Given what I knew of him already, it all figured. As did the faint musty, slightly sweet smell that had arrived in the room with him.

The boy at Thomas's side was his polar opposite. Jonathan was slight and be-freckled, with neatly cut blond hair, and was turned out precisely as I'd anticipated he would be, given he was currently living with a foster family. He was bright as a pin, stiff with new clothes and grooming; only the slight edge of wariness in his expression hinted at the complicated background that I knew lay beneath.

The third child – presumably Chloe – was a beautiful girl. She was somewhat dishevelled, too, a bit like a Disney Cinderella – though presumably not as a result of being on the run around Britain, but simply as a consequence of just being Chloe. Her smile was wide and genuine but her vulnerability was writ large – I wondered how many challenges she had to face just to get productively through the day.

Chloe's hair was long and unruly like Thomas's, though in her case the unruliness took a different form. It was almost white-blonde and stuck out in all sorts of different directions, putting me in mind of candyfloss – the kind given to you on a stick at a fair. On balance, 'unruly' was probably too mild a word for it. I found myself drawn to her immediately.

She was the first to speak. 'Good morning, Miss Watson,' she trilled, directing her high-wattage beam at me, then, without waiting for a reply, gripping both boys by the elbows and more or less manhandling them inside, much to their evident surprise. 'I'm Chloe Jones,' she added. 'I'm the eldest out of all of us. And Miss Vickers has sent us all to do our work with you.'

I closed the door behind them. 'Welcome, all of you. It's very nice to meet you. And first of all, Thomas …' I noticed him stiffen as I said his name. 'Are you sure you're well enough to be in school? That was a nasty bang you had yesterday, even if it didn't need stitches. I was surprised when Mrs Styles told me you'd come in this morning.'

Thomas jerked himself free of Chloe's vice-like grip. 'It's alright, miss,' he said, sweeping a hand up behind his hair, then flipping it up and turning around so I could see the war wound for myself; well, at least a neat square of shaved head around a rectangular dressing. 'I just gotta make sure I don't get it wet.'

'And you're feeling okay?' I asked him.

'I'm feeling fine,' he said, puffing his chest out almost imperceptibly, in what seemed an automatic, almost unconscious gesture, as if to face off anyone who might hint at weakness. I wondered how far his family had come and how he felt about his step-dad.

'Well,' I said, 'you make sure you let me know if you feel funny in any way, won't you? Any way at all, Thomas. Tired or dizzy, headache – anything at all.'

'I'm fine, miss,' he said again. 'It weren't nothing much.'

Well, that was going to be debatable, once Kiara made an appearance, at any rate. In the meantime, I was still conscious that Chloe hadn't put Jonathan down yet. 'Chloe, love,' I said to her, 'why don't you come with me. Since you're the eldest, you can be the first one to choose a tray to keep your things in.'

I held out a hand and she released Jonathan, reaching readily for it instead, reminding me that her touchy-feely nature extended to all human life, including teachers. 'Can I, miss?' she said, as I led her to the cabinet I kept the trays in – the ones where students kept their work and personal belongings, such as pencil cases and whichever card collections were currently the in thing. 'Here we are,' I said. 'Look, there are the pens – can you take them to the table? And the trays have the name tags already inside them, so if you'd like to choose which one you want, then you can go ahead and sit down and write yours, okay?'

This seemed occupation enough for the moment, so I left Chloe to decide on a colour, and turned my attention back to the two boys. I'd yet to have very much to go on with Jonathan; it would mostly be a case of watch and wait with him over the coming days, to try and tease out why his behaviour was on such a marked downward trajectory.

In that respect, Thomas seemed the more straightforward of the two. I decided that he put me in mind of a modern-day Artful Dodger, and not just because of his hair – which badly needed cutting – and his dodgy antics with Kiara the previous day. There was a veneer of confidence about him, a kind of swagger – though so far, at least, not an irritating one; just this aura he had of being able to handle himself. Which would figure, given his circumstances, and the fact that he was markedly big for a 12-year-old, and I knew that his cockney accent – which, again, was Artful Dodger through and through – would confer status on him all by itself.

He didn't yet know that Kiara would be joining us, however, and as I knew she could walk through the door at any moment, I was keen to prepare the ground first.

'Right, boys,' I said, 'let's get some trays done for you as well, eh? Chloe's just getting the pens out, and we'll sit you all over there.' I pointed to the table I'd indicated to Chloe and where she was now settling down at to colour her name in. 'I thought as there's only going to be four of you, you can all sit together. To start with, in any case – we'll have to see how it works out, won't we?'

At which moment, as if spirited there specifically to underline the point, there was a second knock at the door and it opened to admit Kelly and Kiara.

'Speak of the devil!' I quipped, as I watched Kiara's jaw drop.

'What's *he* doing here?' she asked me immediately.

'The same as you are, love,' I said mildly, nodding a greeting to Kelly. 'Just one of life's funny little coincidences. Thomas here is going to be with us for half of the week, and …'

'But I only just got away from him, miss!'

Thomas, for all his confidence, said nothing in response to this. Just looked from me to Kiara and back again, clearly bemused. I could almost see his brain whirring, trying to decide what this unexpected development might mean. Which pleased me greatly, as it hinted that, once separated from a peer group that needed impressing, he'd be much less of a class clown than his previous behaviour had suggested. He was probably also more than a little wary.

'You'd be with Thomas anyway, Kiara,' I pointed out, sensing that she already knew she had the upper hand. 'You're in the same tutor group, aren't you? The only difference is that here you'll be spending a bit more of the day together, which will mean you can put yesterday behind you *all the quicker*, won't it?'

'Excellent point,' Kelly enthused, returning my cheery grin. 'So, well, I'll leave you to it, then, Mrs Watson. And what do you say to Mrs Watson, Kiara?' she prompted before she left.

'I'm sorry I'm late, miss,' Kiara parroted as she shrugged off her rucksack, looking thoroughly miserable, resigned to her lot.

'Right, Kiara,' I said, keen to focus on my group bonding session, 'you've already got your tray labelled so why don't you pop your things in it, then go and take a seat by Chloe over there?' I made the requisite introductions and, once the children were settled round the table, albeit warily, in Thomas and Kiara's case, set about getting the lesson under way. The plan for today was for the group to start getting to know each other, and, hopefully, for the children to begin to form bonds by doing activities that involved them working together.

This wasn't just about creating a sense of family in class either – it was also so that I could start assessing the group dynamic and begin to understand the pecking order that was going to emerge. It always did: in any group (whether in school or the workplace, it was the same) everyone always played their part. There would always be an apparent leader – sometimes two – emerging early, plus that class clown who got their status by making others laugh, and the ones who were more happy being led than leading, be it willingly or slightly resentfully. And at some point, more often than not, a *real* leader would emerge. One who wasn't necessarily vocal about being 'the boss', but who would quietly assess the others and work out how best to manipulate the group to get the best out of them, even if that meant allowing someone else to believe they were the one in charge.

It was an important exercise, generally played out over a couple of weeks, and as I loved group dynamics I found it fascinating. Though, right now, with my relatively small (and, in Chloe's case, relatively transparent) bunch of charges, I'd probably have an inkling by the end of the day. One thing was already clear: Thomas was getting first run at stating his case, quietly filling Jonathan in on his run-in with Kiara the previous day, while Kiara herself, seemingly happy to rely on a non-speaking strategy, was being comprehensively adopted by Chloe, who seemed intent on plaiting sections of her hair.

'Okay,' I said, clapping my hands together to get their attention, 'first up are the interviews I'm going to be doing with you all. Once we've got the morning's activity under way I'm going to be calling you individually to the quiet area, so we can have a chat and I can get to know you a little better. In the meantime, here's what we're doing first.'

I then explained what the morning's activity would comprise: an exercise designed to break the ice and work on their listening and general communication skills. It was an area where lots of kids who came to me struggled, often because they had so much already on their minds that they would 'zone out' of whatever it was they were supposed to be doing. The task was therefore all about listening to one another; telling each other little anecdotes about things that had happened to them, which the listener would transcribe and make the basis for a story of their own. I also explained that I wanted them to illustrate their stories too – both with a picture of their partner, and one of themselves – you could tell so much from how a kid perceived themselves via the medium of drawing.

'A self-portrait,' I clarified. 'Who knows what a self-portrait is?'

Thomas shot his arm up enthusiastically, which was gratifying. 'Miss, I know that one, miss. It's a picture you do of yourself, ain't it?'

'That's right,' I said, tickled once again by his accent. I pointed to the back wall. 'And once they're done they can all go up there.'

'Like mugshots on *Crimewatch*,' he suggested.

'Exactly,' I agreed, noticing Kiara's expression. *Exactly*, I could see her eyes saying.

I called Jonathan for his life-space interview first and he followed me across to the reading area with what looked like genuine enthusiasm. This was good to see and, given the information in his file, unexpected. I'd been expecting an adversarial, antagonistic child.

'I'm 11,' he announced proudly as he sat on one of the big cushions, 'and I live with my foster mummy and daddy.'

Jonathan's file suggested that he operated below average intellectually and, emotionally, had the social age of around seven or eight. And I could immediately tell that this was true. It meant I'd need to ignore his real age as I spoke with him, rather as I would have to do with Chloe.

'Wow!' I said, 'you're a big boy for 11, aren't you? Do you have any brothers or sisters, Jonathan?'

'No,' he said, shaking his head, 'not real ones. It's just me. But there's three foster brothers at home. *And* a baby foster sister. So I share them.'

A pretty busy foster mum then, I thought. 'Have you lived with this family for a long time?' I asked him next. I already knew he'd been in care for six months, but I was keen to get a sense of his own perception.

He gave the question serious thought. 'I think so,' he said. 'I don't get to see my dad much anymore. My real daddy I mean. Not my foster daddy. I see him at weekends when he comes back from work.'

'And do you like school?' I asked. 'Do you enjoy it? Miss Vickers said you'd been having some problems and getting angry just lately.'

He bit his lip and started to twiddle with the cuffs of his jumper. 'I do have problems, miss,' he said eventually. 'It's 'cause I'm stupid, miss. I don't know stuff and I'm rubbish at football, and the other boys make me mad and then I get cross and swear and then I lose my mummy dollars and then I don't get stuff and then I get angry all over again.'

He sighed heavily. It was a long, impassioned speech. This anger about losing rewards was clearly the driving force in his life.

'Tell me about your mummy dollars, Jonathan,' I prompted, and he explained that his foster mum had a cabinet in her kitchen, in which was a box containing treats and small toys. At the end of the week, provided he'd earned sufficient dollars (by doing specific tasks and being helpful) he could spend them on the treats of his choice. A bad day at school could derail this, however, as poor behaviour would result in previously earned vouchers being taken away again, often resulting in him having none left come treat day.

I actually thought it was a great idea; a classic way to incentivise a child to change their behaviour, not via punishment, but by accentuating the positive to give them motivation. Though, at the same time, I was sorry that his school day was included in the system, because, to my mind, what happened in school should, in a case like this one, be dealt with in school. Both carers and teachers were working towards the same goal after all, and I couldn't see the logic in him effectively being punished twice for his small transgressions. Was this the key to his growing frustration? That he'd simply got into a cycle of negative reinforcement? Perhaps all that was needed here was to break it. And in my Unit, he had a fighting chance of doing just that. With no flash points, or clever-clever peers, or bullies, or impatient teachers needing answers, there was simply so little opportunity to be 'naughty'.

'Well, we'll try and help you with that, love,' I said gently. 'You've been a very good boy so far this morning, and I'm going to enjoy getting to know you. You can go back now, sweetie, and carry on with your story. Could you ask Thomas to come over, please?'

As Jonathan made his way back to his new classmate, I glanced over at the girls. They were both busy writing now, having presumably shared their respective stories, and I was tickled to see Chloe reach a hand out now and then, and stroke Kiara fondly on her forearm. I wondered what Kiara was making of it – she didn't draw her arm away – and it seemed I wasn't the only one, either.

'She's a bit funny in the head, that one, ain't she, miss?' Thomas said conversationally, as he settled down beside me on a floor cushion. 'This is a bit of alright, miss,' he added, scooping his fringe from his eyes. 'I ain't never seen a classroom like this before. It's well cool.'

'Thank you, Thomas,' I said. 'But you know –'

'It's Tommy, miss. I didn't like to say before, but it's Tommy. No one ever calls me Thomas 'cept me granny.'

'Okay, Tommy it is, then,' I agreed. 'But, you know, one thing I need to tell you is that we don't name-call in this classroom,' I added mildly.

'I weren't calling her names. I was just saying she ain't right in the head, miss. And he's not, either, is he?' he added, nodding back towards Jonathan. He did a circular motion with his index finger beside his temple. 'Bit away with the fairies, like, isn't he? That's not calling people names, miss. It's just a fact. That's why they're here, isn't it?'

I half-expected him to ask why *he* was here, given that. The old 'why have I been put in with the retards?' being a common refrain, from kids who, in saying so, were answering their own question. But I had detected no cruelty in Tommy's tone, just simple curiosity.

'I know what you mean,' I said, 'and I know what you're trying to say, Tommy, but in this class we have children with *all* kinds of different problems, and we don't use words that mock them, okay?'

'But I wasn't, miss.'

'You don't think saying "away with the fairies" isn't mocking?'

He had the grace to blush at this. 'Aw, well, okay, miss, I s'pose you're right. Anyway,' he added, brightening again. 'What do you wanna know about me?'

'Well,' I said, looking down at the notes Julia had given me, 'according to what I have here, you are coming to me for half the week, and going to your regular lessons for the other half. Do you know why you've been asked to come and spend time with me?'

'Cos I ain't done much school, miss,' he said immediately. 'Since we did a runner from me step-dad, we was never in any place long enough. Mr Clark says I need breaking in gently.'

He grinned then, obviously remembering something. 'Like a horse, was what he said. You can't rush these things can you, miss?'

I almost burst out laughing. If Tommy was trying to sell me the idea that he needed a good long stint on my floor cushions, he was going about it the right way.

'You're absolutely right, love. We can't rush these things. And we shouldn't try to, should we? How are you finding the lessons that you do attend, anyway?'

'Not bad,' he answered, 'but I don't think the teachers like me very much.'

'Nonsense!' I said. 'What's not to like about you, eh? You seem like a perfectly nice young man to me.' I paused then, and leaned closer, so I could speak to him more quietly, and as I did so, I nearly gagged breathing in the whiff of unwashed clothes. I found myself feeling desperately sorry for him all of a sudden. 'Well, when you're not being silly like you were yesterday, anyway,' I reminded him. 'But I think you already know that, don't you? And, if you didn't, I imagine Mr Brabbiner made that clear enough at the hospital, so I'm not going to go over it again now. Suffice to say that while you and Kiara are here together, that's the side of you I expect to see, okay?'

The swagger subsided somewhat. He'd learned a lesson. No doubt about it. 'I know, miss. I won't do it again, miss.' There was a pause. 'Though, miss,' he added, lowering his voice, 'I didn't say all them things she said I did – and nor did Connor. Just so's you know, okay. She weren't telling the truth about that.'

'Are you telling *me* the truth?' I asked him, conscious of the sudden seriousness of his expression. Perhaps she'd over-egged the pudding just a little in her half-awake, hysterical state.

'Honest to God, I am, miss,' he said, putting me in mind of Fagin's gang again.

'*Good*,' I said, 'because that's part of the deal in being here. Anyway, as far as I'm concerned, that subject is closed.

So, Tommy,' I asked him then, 'do you have any brothers or sisters?'

He shook his head. 'No brothers,' he said, looking gloomy. 'I wish I did, but me mam had had enough. I got four older sisters and they're a nightmare, they are.'

I laughed. 'That's girls for you, Tommy. Whatever else do you think we were born for, if not to be nightmares to our brothers?'

At which point the bell rang for mid-morning break, eliciting a fist-pump from Tommy and a cry of 'Yes! Playtime!' and a similarly animated whoop across the room from Jonathan. Chloe and Kiara, in contrast, didn't seem as if they could care less. Which didn't surprise me. In Kiara, Chloe had everything she wanted right there, and I had a strong sense that the feeling might be mutual. Tommy's presence notwithstanding, my mysterious girl seemed almost serene, and I wondered which of these kids would prove the most challenging to help. Would it be the boys, with their seemingly straightforward set of problems, or Kiara? In Chloe, I knew the situation was rather different. In reality, though I would obviously do what I could with her, I was mostly keeping her safe till she could be sent somewhere more appropriate. As for the rest, it was probably too early to say.

Which was fine. I felt a familiar rush of pleasure as I watched my little quartet troop out into the corridor, Tommy first, Jonathan second, the girls together, bringing up the rear. It was perhaps the silliest way of describing things imaginable, so it wasn't something I'd ever share, but it was at this stage that I got the strongest sense that anything was possible; that in the children I'd been given a set of raw ingredients and that working with them as a group was like baking a cake. That together, provided I put my skills to good use, we'd create something even better than the sum of its parts. Well, sort of. I probably just needed another coffee.

Chapter 6

During break, Gary Clark had called in to let me know that Thomas's new timetable had been completed, and this meant that he would spend Mondays, Tuesdays and the first half of Wednesdays with me, and the rest of the week would go to normal lessons.

'We've looked at the schedules and his mum is keen to see him do English, Maths and French – he's apparently very good at languages,' Gary explained. Then he laughed. 'I wonder if she knows much of the language I've heard him using in the corridors since he's been here ...'

'He's not the only one,' I said, 'and I bet he's certainly not the worst offender. I'll let him know after break, then.'

'Did you make any headway with him and Kiara?' Gary asked.

'Kiara doesn't seem in the least bit fazed by any of it,' I told him. 'But I did notice Tommy was keeping his distance. I guess he never expected to be sharing the same class with her, poor kid.'

Gary snorted as he got up to leave. 'Poor kid? I'm not so sure about that. I think young Tommy can hold his own at our school, no worries.'

I was pleased to see that after break the four students returning to me seemed to have spent their break time together. I always liked that. The children that came to me were so often the outsiders – quite literally, sometimes, as well. The ones who hovered at the edges of groups and playgrounds, never quite managing to break in, much less fit in. Not all of them, obviously. Some commanded huge retinues out in the world of 'real' school, but they tended to be the bullies and they did so for all the wrong reasons. This little lot didn't fall into that category, however, and I had high hopes that they'd gain much from each other's company. Had done already, it seemed. There was definitely a jovial atmosphere and they all seemed to be a lot more relaxed.

'Back to your seats then,' I called out above the chatter. 'I took a look at your books while you were out and I see that you've been working well. It's time for you to start working on your self-portraits now though, and remember, these will be going on the wall, so best efforts, please.'

I then pointed to the two long sets of drawers along the side wall. 'All the art materials you'll need are in there so take out what you need and try to keep the drawers tidy.'

I noticed that Chloe was trying, unsuccessfully, to hold Kiara's hand as they walked across to the art materials, so I decided I'd do her life-space interview first, and give Kiara a break. 'Chloe, love,' I called, 'time for our getting-to-know-each-other chat, sweetheart, okay? Let's go sit in the quiet corner, shall we?'

Chloe let go of Kiara's cardigan sleeve, but not before giving it a gentle stroke with her other hand, and then followed me over to the book shelves.

'I love Kiara, miss, she's so pretty,' was the first thing she said to me, as she sat cross-legged on one of the large floor cushions. 'Tommy and Jonathan are nice too. Jonathan said I'm not allowed to call him Johnny, miss. Did you know that? I have another friend called Johnny, miss. I like that name.'

'Well, that works out fine, then, doesn't it, Chloe, because now you won't get them mixed up, will you?' I said, smiling at her as I took the small chair opposite her. 'But anyway, we don't need to worry about that – I want to hear a bit more about you now. Is that okay?'

She nodded, simultaneously trying to pat her unruly hair down. It seemed to be something of a thing with her.

She obviously became aware of it and smiled ruefully at me. 'It's a bit windy out there, miss, isn't it? And Mum forgot to give me a hairbrush. Do *you* have a hairbrush?' She looked at me hopefully. 'Tommy said I look like I've got a bird's nest on my head.'

'Is there just you and your mum at home, Chloe?' I asked her, once I'd assured her that I did.

Chloe nodded. 'Yes,' she said. 'I don't have sisters or brothers. So there's just me to look after Mum.' She paused. 'She's poorly, see, and if I had a sister she'd be able to help, wouldn't she? But I don't. I'd like a sister. I don't think I'm going to get one though.'

I glanced down at my file. It didn't say anything about Chloe's mum having any sort of illness. But then, perhaps it wouldn't. Perhaps her illness was the one I'd already been told about. The one that, sadly, came out of a bottle.

'She's poorly?' I asked Chloe anyway, so I could try to see things through her eyes. 'Oh, I didn't know that, love. What's wrong with your mum?'

She leaned in towards me. 'I'm not s'posed to say, but it's if she doesn't have her Vodka. That's when she gets really sick and she needs my help the most.' Chloe scratched at her scalp before continuing. 'My nan sometimes comes round to help out but I don't like her. She shouts at my mum, miss. Really loud sometimes, and all. She's mean, my nan. It's not my mum's fault she's poorly, is it, miss?'

'No, love,' I soothed. And, in a sense, she had a point. Who chose to be an alcoholic, after all? What was also clear was that talking about her mum was upsetting for the poor child, who seemed to be drawing herself inwards on the cushion. I felt so sorry for this poor, affectionate, probably often bewildered girl. I didn't want to judge her mother because I knew nothing about her, or why she drank, but as I began to take in Chloe's dirty finger nails, wild hair and general air of dishevelment, I couldn't help but feel a little bit of frustration that she should be so neglected. 'Does your nan live close to you?' I asked.

'Just a few minutes away,' she said. 'And my granddad did too, but he died when I was little. I don't remember him much, but my nan used to be much nicer when I was little. She used to give me cuddles, but she just goes off on one now – mainly at my mum, like I said – but at me as well. She says I'm a big girl and I don't need cuddles any more. That's not right, is it, miss? You're never too old for cuddles.'

I wondered where she'd heard that said and my heart really went out to her. I wondered what she went home to every night after school. 'You're right,' I said firmly. 'No one is *ever* too old for a cuddle.'

'Yeah, but now I only have my mum and my teddies.' She looked brighter then. 'And my new friends. I can cuddle my new friends though now, can't I? And maybe you as well, miss?'

'Maybe me as well,' I agreed, leaning forwards to squeeze her shoulder before standing up. 'And you'll get looked after here. And I tell you what. I think I have a spare bobble in my handbag. How about I pop that hair of yours into a ponytail before the lunch break? Right now, though, it's time for you to get on with your picture, while I have a chat with Kiara, okay? Will you send her over to me?'

'Ooh thanks, miss,' she gushed as she too stood up. 'I *love* having my hair brushed.' She fairly skipped away.

I watched Kiara gently untangle herself from the hug Chloe was determined to greet her with, and as she did so I wondered at her patience. For an only child, she had a sweet, older-sisterly air about her; another way in which she seemed that much older than her years.

'You okay, love?' I asked her as she folded herself down onto the floor cushion. 'Not feeling too overwhelmed by affection?'

She shook her head. 'No, it's fine, miss. I don't mind. Well, not most of the time. It's a bit – you know – weird – but I know she doesn't mean any harm. I've seen her round school. I know what she's like.'

'And how are *you*, Kiara? You know, after yesterday. I was a bit worried, but you and Tommy seem to be okay about it all. *Are* you?'

Kiara glanced across at the boys and then shrugged. 'Yeah, I'm fine, I guess. Isn't much choice, is there? And he knows if he tries anything on again I'll batter him.' She sighed. 'It's just boys, isn't it? They're all like that, aren't they?'

I was interested in her world-weary tone. It seemed a strange thing for a girl of her age to say. She was only 12 after all. I racked my brains to try and remember if 12-year-old girls had boyfriends these days.

'I don't know about that,' I said, 'but some certainly are. They'll do anything to get the other boys to laugh at them, and I guess Tommy was just trying to earn himself some points – with him being new to the school, and everything. He probably doesn't have many friends just yet.' I paused for a moment before adding, 'Do you have a boyfriend, Kiara?'

She shook her head. 'No *way*. Why would I want a boyfriend? Boys are idiots.'

'Oh you say that now,' I said. 'My Riley used to say the same thing when she was younger, but now she can't wait to get married. You might change your mind yet. Just you wait and see.'

But I could see our conversation had headed up a blind alley, as Kiara seemed to have turned her attention elsewhere. Typical, I thought, watching her looking intently at something on the bookshelves – try to get some of my kids to read a book (or even *choose* one, in some cases) and you'd get nothing but moans and groans, but sit them down in the middle of them and try to get them to open up and suddenly books were the best things since sliced bread.

'Tell me about what you get up to at home,' I suggested instead. 'Your mum told me that she has to work a lot of hours. So. What do you do with yourself while she's out at work?'

Kiara shrugged again and, as if on auto-pilot, her hand went to her head and she started to pull out single strands of hair. 'I dunno, miss,' she said. 'Watch TV, do my homework, listen to music. Anything really. I sometimes go round to my dad's if I get bored.'

'Ah yes, your mum said you've started seeing your dad again. And after quite a while, I hear. How is that going?'

'Good,' she said firmly. 'He's much more chilled than my mum. Not all stressy all the time, moaning at me if I leave a cup in the sink or something.'

I laughed. It was a familiar refrain from kids when it came to absent parents. The grass almost always seemed greener on the other side, the parent also so much more accommodating. 'Well,' I said, just so she was open to the idea, 'I think all working mums are a bit like that, Kiara. I know I am. When you get home after a hard day, you like your home to be nice and tidy so you can have a rest. Dads never seem quite as fussy about that sort of thing, do they? And if you only see your dad a couple of times a week, he's probably just pleased to see you. So you get along well with him then?'

'I want to live with him,' she said, with sudden firmness. 'And I will, too. Soon as I'm old enough, I'm off. My dad said she can't keep me locked up for ever, and she can't!'

I was shocked by the unexpected edge in her voice. I wondered if she'd had this conversation with her mum. 'Locked up? Come on, love, I'm sure your mum doesn't lock you up.'

'No! Not *really* locked up,' Kiara said, looking at me as though I were getting on her nerves. 'But making me stay with her instead of letting me live with Dad. It's not fair. Why does *she* get to choose?'

I hesitated before answering because the truth was that I didn't know, and I certainly wasn't about to make a guess. 'I suppose it's just because she's your mum, love, and when they split up it was in your best interests to stay put rather than go off with your dad.'

'Yeah *right*,' Kiara replied, her voice full of scorn. 'Anyway, like I said, it doesn't matter anyway. As soon as I'm old enough, I'm off. It's no biggie.'

'Well,' I began, 'that's obviously something for the future, but –'

But Kiara had clearly moved on. 'D'you want me to do Chloe's hair for her, miss?' she said, speaking across me. 'I heard you saying about having a bobble. I could do it for her if you like. I'm good at hair. I do my mum's all the time. She'd probably like it if I do it.'

I was tempted to push it – try to make sense of the seeming contradictions I was hearing; how she wanted to run off to her dad's but how she did her mum's hair for her all the time. But I decided to leave it, at least for the moment – 12 year-old girls were often walking contradictions in themselves.

'I'll bet she'd love that,' I said instead.

Kiara stood up. 'An' then she can come to dinner with me as well.'

I wondered what her situation at home was really like. There was just something – something I couldn't even hazard a guess at. 'That would be nice, love,' I said. 'I'll go and find my bobble, and soon as you're done with your pictures you can sort it out for her.' I smiled. 'Bless her – "sort" being the operative word!'

Kiara grinned. 'Leave it with me, miss,' she said. 'I like a challenge.'

And she rose to it, too. Chloe was soon the proud owner of what I was informed was a 'messy bun'. And, yes, it *was* messy, but it was also the 'in' thing, apparently. And at least a darn sight less messy than it had been before.

So far, I thought, not bad progress at all. Just not quite enough of it, that was all.

Chapter 7

As it turned out I got Tommy full time after all, and in circumstances that made me very glad that I did. Better with me than with some I could mention. It was in the very first week in fact, and the day after I'd returned from my weekly lunch at the new 'Reach for Success' centre. We'd planned a routine, in that I'd go over there every Wednesday lunchtime as that was the day that all the students had to plan a menu, buy the ingredients then prepare and cook a meal for themselves and their teachers. It was a great confidence-boosting exercise, as well as being very useful for them, and it meant that I could spend a good half-hour catching up on progress and get a free meal to boot. Would that every aspect of my job was so agreeable.

There's no rule that everyone you work with has to be your bosom pal. In fact, in the case of a workplace as big as mine was, I'd say the chances of that happening would be extremely small. What was also true was that there were a small minority of the teaching staff whom I didn't really know by name but already knew intuitively that I might not see eye to eye with, just by a combination of instinct and observation – instinct that we were unlikely to have much in common, and the odd thing I'd gleaned, observed or heard in the staff-room that made me aware that not everyone worked the same way.

One such was Mr Hunt, one of the senior chemistry teachers, who'd been at the school almost two decades and was something of an institution. His notoriety was so longstanding that he had even been blessed with a nickname – one based on his real name, the unremarkable 'Richard Hunt', duly shortened and completely unprintable.

He was equally notorious among the teaching staff, as being a man who liked to tell it like it was. Which was fine. Well, up to a point, anyway. The staff-room was a place for staff to unwind and catch up with each other, obviously, so it didn't do to get all uppity about some of the things said behind closed staff-room doors. Teaching was a stressful profession and teachers wouldn't be human if they didn't have the odd exasperated rant about a particularly trying child from time to time – heaven knew, I'd done it myself.

But there was the odd teacher, I'd noticed, who – perhaps because they were getting weary of the daily grind – didn't seem to like many of their pupils much at all. So much so that a more naïve me (one maybe 20 years younger) would have been inclined to question why on earth they even became teachers in the first place. I'd never do that now; it would be the last way to win friends and influence people, after all. And who was I to pass judgement on a teacher who'd been slogging away for 30 years and who, with all the changes on top of the challenges and pressures, was getting to the end of their professional tether?

Mr Hunt, I'd decided, definitely came into that category, or was at least getting palpably close. He was a clever man, an irritable man, a man who didn't suffer fools gladly – a great nurturer of those with a similar spark of academic potential, but less than patient with those who didn't know one end of a pipette from another; as they soon found out, when they had the great misfortune of being skewered on the end of one of his fiery rantathons – something of a legend around school.

So when Gary Clark appeared in my classroom doorway the following Thursday and Mr Hunt's name was mentioned in relation to Thomas Robinson, I think I already knew that perhaps his brand of chemistry lesson would not be the kind in which our newest pupil would be likely to shine. He was altogether too boisterous and inclined to pubescent silliness – silliness being the cardinal sin for Mr Hunt, particularly when there were chemicals and lab equipment around.

'But I have good news to impart first,' Gary said, as he beckoned me out into the corridor, having boomed his usual warm hello to Kelly and the other kids.

'I'm all for that,' I said. 'What is it?'

'Are you free after school today? Only Kiara's mother called first thing to say she'd be happy for you to pop round there. Said you could walk Kiara home from school today if you like.'

'That was quick,' I said. With the 'fuss over nothing' stance Mrs Bentley had largely taken, I'd anticipated a couple of weeks might pass before we heard from her, or even that I'd need to call again.

'If you still want to, that is,' Gary added. 'She finishes work at three today. How's Kiara been since she's been with you, anyway?'

'Still tired,' I said. 'Still drifting off. Still hair pulling when she does so. Happier, though. As far as I can gauge, compared with what various teachers have told me, she definitely seems less stressed in a small group environment.'

In truth, I felt Kiara had settled extremely well. Had it not been for the self-soothing and that odd 'hard-to-put-your-finger-on-but *something*' way she had about her, I'd have felt a bit uncomfortable about keeping her from main-stream lessons; for an otherwise well-adjusted child who liked a quiet, un-taxing life, it was definitely a soft option. But I was still convinced Kiara wasn't that.

'That will be fine,' I said, mentally scrolling through my domestic to do list. If I caught up with my paperwork at lunchtime, I wouldn't even be late home. I'd leave a message for Kieron, though, just in case.

'I'll leave you to let her know, then,' he said. 'I'm assum-ing she'll be receptive? Anyway, Thomas,' he added, once I'd nodded my confirmation. 'I'm afraid this half a week thing doesn't seem to be working out too well. I've already had reports back from two of his teachers yesterday, saying that he's acting up in class. Being generally disruptive, refusing to knuckle down to any work. I think we may have acted hastily and expected too much from him after such a long period away from school.'

'So you want me to have him full time?' I asked. 'That wouldn't be a problem.' It really wouldn't. I rather liked Tommy and, while a return to mainstream classes would get him back on track with catching up the work he'd missed, I did think my Unit would be a better place for him until he'd re-adjusted to the discipline of a regular school routine. Moving halfway across the country, and in such difficult circumstances, had been a major upheaval for him and his family after all.

'Probably,' Gary said, 'he's in a science lesson right now, and since Mr Hunt is one of the teachers who put a complaint in about him, I wondered if you could pop down – you've got Kelly with you all morning, haven't you? – see how he's doing and, if you think it's the right course of action, bring him back here with you and we'll move on from there?'

Children came to the Unit via a variety of routes, but one of the most common was following repeated reports from teachers that a particular child wasn't working well in class. They could either be showing signs of distress, withdrawing, refusing to co-operate, or just proving unmanageable and disruptive. When this happened, Jim Dawson, the other Behaviour Manager, would usually step in and observe for a while, monitoring for a day or two, or even just part of a lesson, to decide whether it was really warranted to move them. Often it was simply a clash of personalities, or, though it was rarely admitted, simply easier and less stressful for the teacher. If this was deemed to be the case then a child would remain in regular class but work would be done with the teacher in question to help them cope better; some extra training in behavioural techniques, perhaps, while being supported by a teaching assistant, who'd sit with and assist the challenging child.

On this occasion, with Tommy already with me for half the week anyway, it made sense for me to go instead of Jim, though. 'Of course,' I said. 'I'll grab my bag and head up there right away. Let's hope he hasn't actually blown anything up yet, eh?'

'Or any*one*,' Gary added. 'Or he'll find himself at the sharp end of an explosion of the Mr Hunt variety.'

We exchanged a look rather than needing to say anything. Not nice.

I didn't often find myself in the science block, so it took a while to track down the classroom in question – which was actually one of the labs and, as I'd been told, currently full of a year eight group of pupils engaged in complicated operations with Bunsen burners.

Chemistry not being my thing, I couldn't have said what they were all doing exactly, but there were goggles involved, as well as an odd metallic smell, and an array of what might conceivably be noxious chemicals, over which various groups of children were bent, like covens of industrious witches over cauldrons, only in lab coats.

Mr Hunt was at the back of the class and it took a moment or two for him to spot me, upon which he strode purposefully back to the front. I smiled as he approached, in response to his eye-rolling, having already decided on the walk over to dispense with observing Tommy's behaviour and just take him back to the Unit with me.

Well, provided Mr Hunt was happy, which I didn't need to be a scientist myself to judge that he probably would be.

'Excuse me, Mr Hunt,' I said as he drew level and lowered further the slim wire-framed glasses he had perched on his nose. 'I've come to collect Tommy. Thomas Robinson?'

'Ah, Mrs ... ah ... Watson. Good, good,' he replied. He took the glasses off completely then and waved them vaguely behind him. 'Good.'

I lowered my voice. 'What's he been up to? Has there been a problem with him today?' I asked, speaking quietly so as not to disturb the mostly industrious class.

Mr Hunt had no such qualms about the volume switch, however. 'Ah, our young master Robinson,' he said in a voice loud enough to get everyone's attention. A voice *designed* to do so, if I wasn't much mistaken. 'Yes, indeed, Mrs Watson,' he continued, wafting his glasses behind him once again. 'There *has* been a problem, so I'd be very grateful if you did just that. Let me see ...' he went on, making a show of scanning the classroom and, if I wasn't mistaken, sniffing the air. 'If you follow the smell, I think you'll find him sitting under some dirty little cloud, just about – ah, there he is – *there.*'

To say I was aghast would be a massive understatement, and as the class, fully attentive now, began whispering and giggling, I wasn't just stunned by Mr Hunt's words, I was appalled. I glared at him as I walked around him and across the room to the end of Tommy's bench. His face and neck were as red as the rubber Bunsen burner gas tubes, and I felt my anger rise. How easy it was to casually humiliate a child.

'You're not in any trouble, Tommy,' I said as I beckoned him to come with me, conscious that a boy just behind him was holding his nose and fanning the air theatrically. I glared at him as well, grateful that at least Tommy hadn't seen him do it. 'I just need your help with something in the Unit, love, that's all. Could you come with me, do you think?'

No such luck, however, as another boy, this time in Tommy's eye-line, was already responding to the theatricals with a snort of suppressed laughter, causing Tommy to wheel around and catch the other boy in the act. 'You fucking *arsehole*!' he spat, kicking out at one of the nearby lab stools and toppling it. 'You're *all* dickheads!' he added, as it landed with a clatter. He turned to the front of the class. 'Especially you, "*sir*"!'

Mr Hunt, who I expected quite enjoyed upping the ante from time to time, didn't seem fazed in the least. In fact, though he spread his palms in a gesture of apparent exasperation, I thought he looked rather pleased with himself. 'See what I have to put up with?' he said to me, as I followed Tommy towards the front, hoping he wouldn't do anything *really* silly. 'Just get the obnoxious little sod out of here.'

I quashed the urge to pass a comment about the obnoxious sod standing right in front of me, and instead walked right past him, just as Tommy thankfully had, saying nothing. 'Come on, love,' I said, once we were almost at the door. 'Let's get you over to my room before you get any angrier, eh?'

I shut the classroom door behind me with unnecessary force, and though I knew I was being childish, I didn't regret it. I was furious. How could a teacher be a fully paid-up member of the school's anti-bullying campaign and at the same time speak to a child in such a fashion? What Mr Hunt had said and done had beggared belief. It would have been bad form enough in the staff-room (well, to my mind, at any rate) but to say such things and to address them to the whole class, to boot, was a disgrace, and I had half a mind to report him.

And to then have the temerity to bemoan what *he* 'had to put up with' when he'd so blatantly provoked it himself! I took a few deep breaths before addressing Tommy, whose expression had changed from one of anger and defiance to one of helplessness, hopelessness and shame.

I put a hand on Tommy's shoulder but arranged my face so it didn't look too maternal or sympathetic. I had a feeling he was close to tears and desperate not to break down. My heart surged for him. 'Come on, sweetie,' I said, briskly guiding him down the corridor. 'I think you can give science a miss for a couple of weeks, okay?'

Tommy didn't speak. Merely nodded as he marched along beside me. I didn't press it. I could tell how much he didn't want to cry in front of me.

Shame on *you*, Mr Hunt, I thought. *Shame* on you. He hadn't heard the last of this yet.

Chapter 8

For all that I wanted to have a few words with Mr Hunt, it was Tommy who I naturally felt obliged to have a stern word with as we made our way back to my classroom. Which did the trick. Almost as soon as I gently upbraided him about his language, his face properly crumpled and this time he did cry.

Which made me feel even worse. And since he was already in tears, I had no compunction about putting an arm around him now.

'I'm sorry, miss,' he sniffed, pulling a bit of sweatshirt cuff down over his hand and using it to wipe his face. 'I don't mean to shout an' that, but I can't help it. Me mum would go *mental* if she knew I was putting up with stuff like that and not sticking up for myself.'

'And you should stick up for yourself,' I agreed. 'Your mum's right about that. But there's ways and ways,' I went on, making a mental note about the ways I might choose to make my own point to Mr Hunt.

'You don't know what it's like, miss,' Tommy said, recovering his composure a little. 'She really means it. That's what she tells us all the time – that we mustn't let anyone treat us bad, *ever*. That she didn't take years of beatings just for us to end up the same. Honest to God, miss, she'd swipe me one. She would!'

I thought it best not to point out the contradiction in what he'd said, not only because I felt a rush of warmth for Mrs Robinson, but also because I completely got where she was coming from; even though I'd not yet met her, from what I'd seen of Tommy so far, I could tell she was a woman who, having lived with fear and violence, was keen to raise her kids to look out for themselves so they didn't end up in the same boat.

It wasn't always that way. From what I'd seen in school, and from the vulnerable adults I'd worked with in my last job, for every woman like Tommy's mum (who I'd visualised in my head as a no-nonsense, Boudicca-like character) there was another that was too broken, too cowed, to be that robust. The children of these mums reacted to the violence they'd witnessed as their mums did, by being nervous, highly anxious and afraid.

I didn't blame them or judge them. They were all victims of domestic violence – a pernicious canker in society whose effects spread far and wide. Tommy, I decided, was probably one of the lucky ones, in that his mother had found the wherewithal to get physically right away. Yes, he'd missed some schooling, but I thought he'd be okay. To have got away from such a situation, and to have started a new life, would most likely have empowered his mum to be determined that her kids would live differently, and Tommy would surely be better off for it. He simply needed to learn how to handle himself more appropriately.

'I can understand that,' I conceded, 'but, Tommy, you just can't lash out, with your fists *or* your tongue. Certainly not in school, or you'll end up getting excluded permanently and we don't want that, do we? I think you just need to learn how to cope better in stressful situations.'

But Tommy wasn't to be mollified. 'What?' he huffed. 'Even though the teacher is acting like a dick?'

I couldn't help but sympathise. In fact, I wished I could find some clever riposte to slip him; something that would have had the class laughing *with* him rather than *at* him. Of course, I didn't, because to involve myself in such subversive behaviour would be to set off down a very slippery slope – the staff were supposed to present a united front, after all. So instead I sighed sympathetically and said nothing to Tommy. Just made a mental note that I had unfinished business with a certain Mr Hunt.

We returned to the classroom to find it was proving to be a productive morning. I'd not been gone long, but a great deal had been achieved in my absence – unsurprising, since I've yet to meet a child in a classroom who wasn't happy to be creating some sort of art. I'd have liked us to be contributing something else to the Easter assembly, too – a group poem recital, perhaps, or a song – but with my little group so new there wasn't the time to choose and rehearse anything, plus I wasn't sure any of them had the confidence to stand up in front of their peers. Perhaps next term, with whoever was still with me.

In the meantime, Tommy was only too happy to don his art apron and get stuck in and, having been greeted by Chloe as warmly as if he had just returned from an Arctic expedition, he was soon looking cheerful again.

My focus now returned to Kiara. 'You okay, love?' I asked her as I took a look at her various creations; like the child herself, the array of eggs were all pretty and neatly executed.

She nodded. 'I like painting,' she said. 'You can lose yourself when you're painting, can't you?'

It was a bit of pocket philosophy, and I wondered whether she'd heard it said, or had realised it herself as a part of the process. I agreed that you could. 'By the way,' I said, 'I'll be walking home with you later, if that's alright by you. Your mum's said I can visit so we can have a proper chat about things. See how we can best help you to get back to your usual self.'

Again she nodded, and agreed that it would be fine for me to do that, but there was something – a flash of something like fear in her eyes. It was gone – or covered up? – in the blink of an eye, too. But not so fast that I didn't see it. What *was* it with this girl?

Rather than the lesson I had originally been planning for that afternoon, I decided that we'd do some work on conflict resolution instead, mostly for Tommy's but for all of their benefit. It was no big deal to do so; being flexible and reactive to issues and situations was, I'd begun to realise, integral to my job. And not just so I could use a situation one of the children had experienced in order to illustrate some aspect of personal growth. It was also because things could be fine in the Unit one minute and the next all hell could break loose. When that happened, any carefully laid plans went to pot, and alternative tasks and lessons needed to be found. I had therefore learned to be savvy, and to have lesson plans for all eventualities; like the best military generals, I always had a back-up plan.

The worksheets I had made up for this afternoon's chosen lesson consisted of a well-known scenario in any school, and consisted, in essence, of just four questions. They were simple questions, too, the first of them being: *'Someone who doesn't really like you is teasing you in front of all your friends. They call you a name that they know will upset you. What do you say and what do you do?'*

The idea was that the child would write down their responses, then answer the next question: *'What happens then?'* That done, they'd be asked to reflect on the consequences of their response, answering a third question: *'What happens next?'*

This step was designed to help them think about ramifications; how the original act and response to it affected people around them – their parents, the teachers, their friends.

Finally, the worksheet asked: *'Are you happy with this outcome? If not, what do you wish would have happened and if you had the chance to do it again, how could you have handled it differently?'*

Whenever I had used this same worksheet in the past it had had the desired outcome. Each child was forced to reflect on something that they would have surely experienced, and really think about the consequences of their actions and those of others. It seemed to be a simple yet enlightening exercise and their answers never failed to impress me. Today was no different, each had obviously thought carefully about it and I had to smile when I saw Tommy's reflective paragraph.

'So the geezer called me stinky but instead of getting shirty about it when everyone laughed, I should have just laughed and said, "Not guilty, sir, Harry Evans has just farted and I think he followed through".'

Not exactly what I had in mind, but at least he saw that by turning the tables he could have avoided some of the humiliation. Putting this into practice, however – well, that remained to be seen.

As the final bell of the afternoon went, the students, as usual, couldn't wait to get out of the classroom and into the warm, spring sunshine. Within a minute there was only Kiara left behind.

'Will you be having tea with us, miss?' she asked shyly, and I noticed she was once again tugging, seemingly unconsciously, at a long strand of hair. Did she hope I'd say I was or that I wasn't?

'No, love,' I said. 'Just a quick "hello" visit, that's all. I like to try and meet with as many of my Unit parents as I can,' I explained. 'Just to help us all get to know each other a little better. Nothing for you to worry about,' I finished, sensing her anxiety was building, and wondering if I should touch her arm to stop her winding her hair round her finger.

She removed it herself then, to haul on her backpack while I shouldered my satchel. 'Off we go, then,' I said brightly. 'You lead the way, we don't want to keep your mum waiting, do we?' Given how terrifically busy she is, I thought but didn't say.

Kiara and her mum lived only ten minutes away from school in a very sought-after area with broad tree-lined streets and manicured gardens. It was very easy to imagine that it was all peace and tranquillity and that all the children played out in their Sunday best.

As we walked there I tried to get her chatting. 'So, your mum has changed her hours then? I guess you see a lot more of her now, don't you?'

Kiara glanced up at me and then immediately looked away. 'Um, yes, I suppose so,' she muttered, head down. 'Did she tell you that?' she added, after a pause.

I sensed a growing unease in her. Was this a normal response to getting home, or just because I was going with her? I wished I could get some sense of what was ailing this mysterious child. 'No, I think it was Mr Clark who told me that,' I clarified. 'But she must have changed some of her hours otherwise she wouldn't be at home now, would she?'

'I s'pose,' she said, as if her mum's working hours were something of a mystery. Which was odd. Surely she had a rota of some sort? Surely she kept her daughter abreast of her movements, in the time-honoured 'I'll be working till X o'clock this evening. Pop the shepherd's pie in the oven, see you in a bit' kind of way?

Or perhaps not. 'When do we break up for the Easter holidays, miss?' Kiara asked me. She really didn't seem to want to talk about home. And that was fine.

'About a week and a half, love,' I told her. 'And then you have two whole weeks off. Won't that be nice?'

Kiara smiled properly then, and as she did so her pretty little face lit up. I was struck once again by how beautiful she was when she was animated like this. 'I can't wait, miss,' she said.

'Me neither,' I agreed. 'What have you got planned? Anything nice?'

As I spoke I reflected on her apparent lack of friends, which was something that really concerned me. How did this perfectly personable child get to be such a loner? It wasn't as if she lacked social skills, or had difficulty relating to people. Chloe adored her, and she responded so patiently to her, so it wasn't as if she lacked empathy. Yes, some kids were natural loners, and happy to be so, but this girl just didn't seem to fit that mould. She seemed a girl who'd have a best friend that she took through school with her. A BFF to share secrets with, paint her nails with, go to town shopping with. Or did her mum fill that role for her? From what I'd seen and heard so far, I didn't think so.

She answered immediately. 'Yes, I'll get to see my dad loads,' she said, and the tone in her voice – one of excitement – was unmistakable. She clearly thought a lot about her father, despite (or perhaps even related to) the problems her parents had with each other. 'Here we are,' she added, coming to a stop outside a house midway down the road we'd been walking along, and pushing open a small iron gate.

I turned and took it in, making a quick forensic sweep over the area. There was a neat square of garden, full of neatly trimmed bushes and packed full of flowers – the last of the daffodils and crocuses, the first of the tulips, and some other bright flowers I didn't recognise, with a path down the middle leading to a white, uPVC front door. It was a small semi, and had what looked to be brand new windows. They might not have been, but gleamed so spotlessly that it was difficult to imagine otherwise, and all sported identical bright, white nets, all tied back from the centre with equally snowy ribbon.

As first impressions went, it hinted at the sort of domestic perfection that I had to confess to aspiring to myself, even though, at times, it drove my family round the bend.

And if I was impressed with the outside, I was positively green with envy when Mrs Bentley opened the door and ushered me inside. Again, I did a quick sweep to try and get a sense of Kiara's mum, this time taking in another set of variables. This woman, who looked to be in her late thirties, obviously liked the finer things in life. Her make-up was immaculate and she had the same elfin features as her daughter; she was strikingly good looking. Her clothes looked as though they'd been bought at some expensive boutique – I'd not seen their like in any of the chain stores I shopped in. Wearing a slim black pencil skirt, a crisp floral blouse and floaty black cardigan, she put me in mind of a solicitor or a magistrate, and straight away I felt slightly intimidated. She worked in a care home? Then she must surely be some sort of manager. Otherwise, it just didn't compute – because though I had no idea whether there was a particular dress code for a care assistant at the home she worked at, surely comfortable clothes would be the order of the day.

'Ah, Mrs Watson,' she said, appearing relaxed and pleased enough to see me. 'Please come through,' she added, smiling. 'It's so nice to put a face to the voice, don't you think?'

I let Kiara step through the small porch before me and waited a moment while she immediately took off her shoes and placed them neatly on a wooden rack alongside other female footwear. I bent down to unbuckle my sandal to follow suit but Mrs Bentley immediately stopped me. 'Oh please, it's fine, honestly,' she assured me. 'I'm sure you haven't been trudging through muddy fields on your way here! Come on, come on through.'

I followed, but not before I noticed the look of consternation on Kiara's face, staring at my feet as if she couldn't quite believe what she was seeing. I smiled ruefully. I had been guilty of exactly the same behaviour in the past –

telling Riley and Kieron to remove their shoes on pain of death and then pretending to other visitors that, actually, I wasn't a fussy housekeeper at *all*. Oh, I knew where this woman was coming from.

Kiara's mum led me into the kitchen, and that's when I really began to take in the full impact of my surroundings and what they might signify. Everything that had initially impressed me – the minimalistic chic of the place, the absolute spotlessness – was now starting to make me feel slightly uncomfortable. Not only wasn't there a single item out of place, there was also a distinct lack of the sort of items that made a house (particularly one containing a 12-year-old) a home. Admittedly, I was a clean freak – I knew that well, and had learned to live with it – but this level of clean-freakery was, well, freakish. At a guess, this was a level bordering on being a bit OCD, which, though often said in jest, was no laughing matter. I knew because I'd dealt with kids and adults afflicted with it.

I glanced at the nets – exactly seven pleats in each, and so precise that they almost looked measured, and to the millimetre. The tea towels, coloured to match the pale peach and white of the kitchen cupboards, were neatly rolled and stacked in a pyramid shape at the side of the sink, and there was nothing on show anywhere but a selection of chic kitchen appliances, which looked almost like they'd been curated for a museum exhibition. A dream kitchen? Or over the top, even by my exacting standards? It looked markedly less lived-in than a just-decorated show-home – at least when dressing a show-home they made it looked like humans were occasionally at home. This was practically clinical.

'Do you eat early?' Mrs Bentley asked me. 'You're welcome to stay for tea, if so.'

I wondered where she might magic a meal from. The only ingestible thing in evidence seemed to be a single lime on the window-sill, and my hunch was that it would be bound for a gin and tonic.

'Oh no, but thank you so much for asking,' I answered. 'My brood eat around five o'clock and I'm under strict instructions to make Hunter's chicken and salad for them tonight.' I wasn't sure why I felt the need to tell her my precise dinner plans, but there was something about the atmosphere that needed filling up, somehow. 'I'd love a coffee though, if you have some, or a cup of tea.'

Kiara was still looking bemused in the doorway, and Mrs Bentley now turned towards her. 'Go on, Kiara,' she said. 'You look like you're catching flies, standing there with your mouth open. Go up and get changed. Don't forget to hang your skirt up and put the tops in the laundry basket. I'm going to have a chat with Mrs Watson here, so hurry along,' she finished, making a little shooing gesture with both her hands.

Kiara smiled at me, looking distinctly nervous, before leaving. I then heard her feet on the stair treads as she ran up the stairs.

'Coffee it is, then,' Mrs Bentley said, filling the kettle, then, having done so, grabbing a cloth from under the sink so she could rub away the drops of water from the worktop.

She then pulled out a chair from under the tiny kitchen table, and urged me to sit on it. 'So,' she said, 'I assume you've got more questions about Kiara. Is that right?'

I duly sat down. 'Yes – well, I mean, what I'd really like to do is chat. About the hair pulling – which she's still doing. Are you aware of her doing it much at home? And – well, whether there's anything else you've noticed. Anything you're concerned about. And her dad,' I added, as she pulled identical mugs from a cupboard. 'I have been wondering about her relationship with her dad, and how that's affecting her. I know you said that he doesn't take on much of a role with her, but she really does seem quite fond of him. How are things in that area?' I finished, watching for her reaction.

There seemed not to be one. 'Instant alright?' she asked. I nodded. She duly got some out – from another cupboard, rather than from a canister on the worktop – and proceeded to make the drinks, leading to further enquiries about milk, and then sugar, and if so, how much of each.

It wasn't until this task was completed that she opted to answer. Thinking time, perhaps?

'I don't know what to tell you about the hair pulling,' she said once she'd sat down herself, carefully placing her mug on a coaster. The kitchen table, inexplicably, was dressed with a white tablecloth, as if sitting in a Michelin starred restaurant rather than a small suburban kitchen. I didn't imagine she and her daughter were the kind to sit down and eat pizza together on it, that was for sure. Then I checked myself. Appearances could be deceptive.

'I really don't know what to say about it,' she added, sighing. 'I'm still convinced it's an attention-seeking ploy. She never does it at home. *Never*. So, to my mind, it must be to do with something that's going on in school.' She looked pointedly at me. 'Are you *sure* she isn't being bullied?'

I shook my head. 'I don't think so,' I said. 'Not that anyone's ever noticed anyway, and I'm sure we'd know about it if she were. We try to be very proactive about that sort of thing. How about friends, though? She seems such a solitary girl. Does she talk about friends? Have them home for tea? That sort of thing?'

'Not these days,' Mrs Bentley said, shaking her head. 'Though she did have a little friend for a couple of years. Samantha her name was. They lived in each other's pockets for a long time. I don't know what happened but they must have had a fall-out, oh, let me see ... six months ago it must have been.'

'Did she tell you why?' I asked, knowing how girls could have such cataclysmic friendship crises.

Mrs Bentley shook her head again. 'No, she didn't. They just stopped hanging out. I did ask, but well, you know what my daughter's like, Mrs Watson. If she doesn't want to talk about something she won't. And it wasn't as if she seemed distraught, because she didn't. Quite the opposite. You have to realise, she's always been a quiet child.'

'So there's nothing you've noticed lately?'

'There really isn't. So I don't really know what to tell you.'

'What about her dad, then? How are things with him?'

'Oh, when it comes to him there is *plenty* that I can tell you.'

She was instantly more animated and I braced myself for a tirade about her ex. And I got one. 'That girl's got rose-tinted glasses when it comes to that man. He's an absolute waste of space. Never helped us financially – he can't get off his backside long enough to find a job for a start. And if it wasn't for her pushing to see him, he wouldn't even bother with her, whatever she likes to think. I'm telling you, he's no father, never has been and never will be. He's good for nothing, that man.'

I had barely gathered my thoughts enough to make a sufficiently non-contentious reply, when a whirlwind entered the kitchen, in the shape of Kiara, dressed in what looked like a pair of pyjamas, returned from her room and clearly in high dudgeon. 'Just you stop that!' she screamed at her mother. 'Why do you always have to bad-mouth my dad? He doesn't do that about you, *ever*, and you're *horrid*! Just because you hate him doesn't mean I have to. I *hate* you!'

I stared at Kiara, shocked. Though I'd heard her launch both barrels at Tommy the first time I'd met her, she was always polite and respectful of teachers, and I really didn't think she was the type of child who would speak to adults like this. Mrs Bentley, however, seemed completely unfazed, so I recalibrated my thinking. Some kids were angels in school and the very devil at home. And vice versa – you couldn't second guess it.

'Kiara, sweetheart,' Mrs Bentley said, calmly, 'I told you to go to your room and that I needed to speak with Mrs Watson. Snooping around and listening in to grown-up conversations will only get you into trouble.' She then gave her daughter a clear warning look. 'Go on. Do as you're told. I said room, Kiara, *now*.'

Kiara, crying freely now, gave me a quick, helpless-looking glance, before turning on her heel and flouncing from the room. It was the kind of exchange between mother and daughter that has doubtless been played out in such circumstances for centuries, and would doubtless carry on being played out as well. I decided it was time for me to leave, because I didn't think there was any more I could usefully do or say, and it wasn't as if I had learned anything I didn't already know. I stood up and picked up my bag. 'I better get going,' I said, anxious to convey by my light tone that I understood how things stood. 'It was lovely meeting you, Mrs Bentley – lovely to put a face to a name, as you said – not to mention seeing your beautiful home.'

'Likewise,' Mrs Bentley said, standing up also and offering me a hand to shake. 'And sorry about that –' she rolled her eyes towards the ceiling. 'You know how things can get when they're that age, I'm sure. Please feel free to call again, won't you? Oh, but do phone in advance to check I'll be home. I've managed to alter a few of my shifts, as I told your Mr Clark, but I've had to agree to provide cover if anyone is off ill or anything, so I might get called in at short notice.'

'I will do,' I said as I opened the porch door. 'And thank you for the coffee. Will you say goodbye to Kiara for me? Tell her I'll see her tomorrow?'

Mrs Bentley agreed and stood by the door as I walked down the path and up the road towards the school, where I'd left my car. And as I walked I reflected on the little outburst I'd just witnessed. Perhaps Mrs Bentley was half right; perhaps Kiara's hair pulling and drifting off were simply symptoms of her distress at the dire state of her parents' relationship. With her mum so censorious about her dad, and Kiara loving him so much, she was bound to feel torn about where her loyalties should lie. It was a nasty situation and one which the poor child should never have been brought into. And it could be, probably would be, nothing more than that. Which made the business of helping her reasonably straightforward.

But if that were so, why, oh *why*, was my brain screaming *no!* at me so loudly?

Chapter 9

Though I mulled over my brief visit to Kiara's home all the way back to school, and then again as I drove the short journey home, by the time I got there I wondered if I wasn't scratching an itch that was mostly in my mind.

It wouldn't have been the first time; I knew I had a tendency to over-analyse – that was my nature, and one of the reasons I'd jumped at the job running the Unit. When 'behaviour' is in your job title, it kind of goes with the territory to spend half your time analysing exactly that.

But as the days passed, and we reached the start of the Easter holidays with nothing of note occurring (not in the sense of ringing alarm bells), I began to convince myself that whatever the reason for Kiara having presented to me as a child in need of extra support, the support we were giving her was reaping rewards. She was a model pupil, too – yes, she still came into school tired and slightly tense at times, but within the cocoon of the Unit classroom she seemed to be having her needs met, and, at the same time, proving a real positive in Chloe's life, which, in turn, fed back into her own sense of self-worth.

And as for the boys – well, they were boys, and of a certain age and persuasion, and both were benefitting from having some lessons in personal development, away from the many triggers and flashpoints of normal school life – something that was key in them adjusting to their different situations and having the tools to cope with the challenges they brought. Jonathan, in particular, had been a real revelation, making me surer still that he'd just got locked into chronically low self-esteem – I made a mental note to speak to Gary about chatting to his foster mum about not using the points chart for anything that happened at school.

All told, it was a productive quartet in the Unit currently, so I skipped off to enjoy the Easter holidays in positive mood. I also had something of a mission in mind. Mike and I had been house hunting for a while now, for no reason other than that I fancied a change. This happened to me quite frequently – there was something of the gypsy in my soul – and was the main reason I'd always preferred to rent rather than buy.

'Itchy feet' was what my mother called it, invariably rolling her eyes when she mentioned it, so the gypsy in my soul clearly hadn't come from her side. Put me in the same location for more than a year or two and, sure as night follows day, I'd soon be pestering Mike to go somewhere else. It was a standing joke in our family that we never got to put up the Christmas tree more than once in any house.

Though I wasn't having that. It was rubbish – I could count at least three places where we'd done this. Still, when my mind was made up …

I usually started by throwing in the odd complaint about the current property, just to set the ball rolling; set out my stall, so to speak. I'd suddenly announce that the garden was either too big or too small, or I'd grumble about the size of the dining room or lack of a conservatory – any perceived 'defect' that I laid eyes on, basically.

Mike and the kids had grown accustomed to this by now, and would always roll their eyes (just like my mum did), shake their heads and then realise that however much they groaned about the prospect, before long we'd be moving house again. We never went far; always remaining close to the schools and our various friends, so nobody *really* minded. And, truth be known, once the process was properly under way, the kids would get excited too, proving my restless gene had been passed on to them.

This was one such time, and the Easter holidays gave us the opportunity we needed to really get stuck into viewing properties and searching the internet for something that struck my fancy. Mike had booked a week off and Kieron was off from college so, as far as I was concerned, there were no excuses to dither either.

On this occasion, however, it seemed my kids had other plans. 'Mum, I swear if I have to look at one more house I'm going to go nuts!' Kieron announced when I was running around the front room with the local newspaper, assuring everyone that this time I had found *the* perfect place. 'The last *three* flipping houses have been perfect,' he moaned on at me irritably. 'Can't I *please* just leave it to you and dad this time, please? Honest, Mum, you're driving me *mad*!'

Much as Kieron disliked change from routine (all a part of his Asperger's) he was actually used to this process by now, and, in my defence, I always went back to what the doctor had told me when he was younger, that while I shouldn't stress him needlessly, it was also important to challenge his various 'security blankets' in order to prepare him for the travails of adult life.

But he clearly didn't want to be part of the decision-making process, and perhaps I needed to rein in just a bit. 'I know how he feels, love,' Mike added loyally, 'and to be fair, he shouldn't have to if he doesn't want to; Riley doesn't have to, does she? Because she's out at work. No, Kieron,' he said, before I had a chance to push another set of details under my son's nose, 'you go off with your mates or something and enjoy your time off. Me and your mum will sort this one out.'

'Charming!' I huffed, though, actually, I *did* take his point. 'Well, just don't either of you be moaning after the fact, then,' I finished, putting down the newspaper and heading off to find my shoes so I could – all being well and a 30-second phone call confirmed it – drag Mike round my newest perfect prospect then and there.

And it was perfect; a beautiful little bungalow with a big bedroom downstairs, and two further ones – his 'n' hers – nestled in the roof. It also sported a big front garden,

mostly laid to hard-standing – handy for extra cars and visitors – and a back garden to die for, with both a cherry tree
in it and the cherry on the top adjacent to it, in the form of
a massive conservatory that led out on to the 'must have' of
the moment: a great expanse of decking that I knew Alan
Titchmarsh would approve of.

'So you see?' I explained, as we headed off to see it in
person. 'It's going to be perfect in every way.'

Mike sighed the sigh of a man who knew there was probably no arguing with me. 'Have you got shares in the
bloody estate agents, woman?' he said instead.

I was right, of course. By the time the Easter holidays had
finished, we'd not only eaten half our combined body
weight in chocolate, we'd also signed up to take over the
bungalow in six weeks' time, which fitted in perfectly for
the half-term holiday. I couldn't wait, and went back to
work with a determined spring in my step and a smile of
happy anticipation (all that lovely clearing out and cleaning
up to look forward to) etched on my face.

It was a winner all round, in fact, as it was practically
across the road from Kieron's college, and also had a bus
stop 20 yards from the front gate that would ensure an
extra five minutes in bed every morning.

Till then, it was sleeves up and time to re-focus on work
and my small but engaging little quartet. Or, rather, quin-
tet-to-be, as one of the first things Gary Clark told me
when I got to work (super-early) was that there was a new
child potentially joining me.

'I'll fill you in more fully later, though,' he said, 'as I don't have all the details yet. All I know is that she's another one who's new to the school. I believe Mike's going to meet with the family first and we'll go from there.'

Mike Moore being the headteacher, who didn't usually do the introductions with new pupils; that task generally fell to the deputy head, Don. Either way, there would be some reason why the girl was being considered for the Unit before she'd even started, something I'd find out in the fullness of time. I was happy for her to join us anyway – I could easily accommodate half a dozen children or more, if needed, and a new pupil always added something to the dynamic. In the meantime, since Kiara hadn't yet turned up at school, I thought I'd start the day with a good deed, and give Chloe a quick make-over, following my first 'domestic rationalisations' over the weekend.

'Come here, sweetie,' I called to her as she trotted into the classroom after the second morning bell, 'I've got a couple of things over here that I think you might like.'

I'd already been unpacking my satchel and now I delved deeper, pulling out a set of old curling tongs, a mirror and a big hairbrush, all the while watching her eyes growing wider at this unexpected Mary Poppins trick. 'According to my daughter, Riley,' I told her, uncurling the lead from the tongs, 'these things can do wonders with frizzy hair. Can make you look like a little princess, or so I'm told. What do you think? Because I thought we might give them a bit of try-out on you, Chloe. Would that be okay?'

There was little doubt that it would be more than okay. 'Oh *yes*, miss, it definitely would be, miss,' she told me, beaming. 'My Auntie Koreen has some of those and she looks *beautiful*. Can you make my hair pretty like hers? Are you *allowed* to?'

I jumped straight on this, having never heard any mention of an aunt before. 'Course I'm allowed to,' I told her. 'And, hey, what about this auntie of yours? Does she help you do your hair sometimes?'

'I don't really remember,' Chloe said chattily. 'I haven't seen her since I was little. I just saw them in some holiday photos.'

'She doesn't live nearby then?' I asked, alert to any possible support out there. This was a niece, after all – and perhaps a cherished one?

But Chloe shook her head. 'She lives in Spain,' she said. 'And my mam says she doesn't know she's born. I don't think they like each other very much. What's don't know you're born mean anyway?'

So not a great deal to build on there, I decided, as I plugged in the curling tongs. Though had there been, the school probably would have known yonks ago. Well, we'd just do our best then. And right now, I'd do my best with her candyfloss hair. I had no idea about the protocol with matters of hair and make-up, nor indeed whether tonging Chloe's hair might breach some health and safety order, but since we'd spent three days at the end of the previous term working in what had felt like Arctic temperatures, I felt I'd be on pretty safe ground if someone tried to tick me off.

Besides, not asking anyone's permission first was a tried and tested strategy – if it turned out I was wrong, I could simply plead dumb.

'Well, here goes nothing,' I assured her, once I'd tried to make some sense out of 'don't know you're born' with her, and possibly failing. 'And, yes, I will do my very, very best. You'll look even more pretty than you are already,' I added, which made her smile light up even more. I glanced over at the boys, who were working on their daily diaries and paying us no attention whatsoever. I usually had them work on dairies first thing every morning, writing about anything noteworthy that might have happened the previous day, or, in this case, anything that might have happened over the Easter holidays, meaning they'd probably have more than usual to write. 'Boys, when you're done with those,' I told them, 'you can take out your Maths workbooks and do the next three pages, please – until Mrs Watson's beauty salon closes.'

The boys groaned predictably, but also good-naturedly, while Chloe clapped her hands together, obviously thrilled to have been singled out for this unexpected treat. And I soon had her hair looking relatively tamed and neatly curled into Bo-Peep style ringlets, which I then gathered into a bobble to make a ponytail.

'Look, boys!' she gushed, flicking up her bouncing curls once I'd finished. 'Just look how pretty I am! Do you like it?'

The boys gave another grunt, this time to express mild affirmation – the making of any more gushing a gesture obviously being tantamount to a proposal of marriage.

'She does look lovely, doesn't she, Tommy?' I prompted. 'Doesn't she, Jonathan?'

'Yeah,' Tommy said. 'Like that mermaid doll my sister used to have off that Disney film.'

'Oh, Tommy,' Chloe trilled, 'you mean Ariel! I do, I look like the Little Mermaid, don't I! I do, don't I, Jonathan?'

Jonathan shrugged. 'I dunno. I don't even know who that is. But yeah,' he finished. 'Yeah, you look alright.'

Once again I was struck by the world according to Jonathan. He'd come to school accompanied by a fat file, bristling with annotations, and now I'd had the chance to delve further into his past, I'd learned that up until he'd been brought into care, he had never learned how to play, didn't own any toys and had no idea about what all the other kids were talking about when they discussed favourite TV shows or movies. I thanked God for that neighbour who had found him scavenging in her bin for food and decided to phone social services. What sort of adult might he have become had she not?

Speaking of which, I thought, as I closed the salon and put the still-warm tongs out of harm's way, I wondered what mysteries would accompany our newest pupil when she came. I'd be glad to have her. It was a good time to bring in a new student, as the four I had were all now at ease with each other; possibly too comfortable in their small, safe, familiar environment, when what they needed to be was robust enough to cope when they returned to the bustle and conflict of a normal classroom setting. And speaking of which, we were still a person short. Where was our other enigma, Kiara? Might she be ill? If so, perhaps her mum had phoned in.

At break time, I was just on my way to reception to find out when I bumped into Gary Clark in the corridor. 'I have news,' he said. 'Looks like you will be getting that new girl. D'you want to pop into my office and I'll fill you in?'

I said yes, and turned around, Kiara's absence temporarily on the back burner, and took a seat beside Gary's Big Boss desk.

'Morgan Giles,' he said, flipping open a manila folder. '15 years old. But no form of regular education whatsoever. She's a gypsy girl,' he added. 'Though I think we refer to them as a traveller these days, don't we?'

'Don't ask me,' I said, shrugging my shoulders. I might have had gypsy in my soul but mine was strictly of the 'painted caravan pulled by a trusty shire-horse' variety, so beloved of children's authors and illustrators. '15?' I said. 'Wow. So she'll be going into year 11. No formal education at *all*?'

'Not as provided by the state,' he said. 'But she's certainly not uneducated. Mike says she's very bright, in fact. And confident with it. Though she won't be able to go into any formal year group. In fact, the family – as in Mr Giles, and her grandmother, who goes by the name of Granny Giles and also lives with her – don't really want her in school at all. It's Morgan who's insisting on it apparently. They've recently moved onto the council caravan site just off the Groves estate. Do you know it?'

I shook my head, though I knew 'of' it all too well. I've never actually been there, but you couldn't help but hear lots about it; as with pretty much any town or city anywhere there was a seemingly endless battle between the councillors, the local residents and the travellers themselves about who had which rights and which won over all the others, with plenty of factions and fights along the way. I'd also heard that it was a dirty place, a dangerous place, and that parents warned their children to keep away from it; that it was next to the landfill site, full of mangy horses and vicious dogs and, perhaps predictably, that lots of bad things happened there. It was just your everyday kind of idle gossip – possibly all of it unfounded – but even so, I'd never felt inclined to go and check myself.

'Well, that's where they live,' Gary went on, 'having moved back there from Newcastle because Morgan has announced that she wants to sit some GCSEs. Maths, English and possibly Geography, apparently. However, Mr Giles is strongly opposed to the idea. He hates our schools – no bones about it – and has always had some kind of tutor for his daughter. Who, I might add, he is adamant is "more than adequate for her needs, being a girl".'

He'd put the last bit in finger quote marks and I pulled a disapproving face.

'Well, exactly,' Gary said. 'And I'm paraphrasing, obviously. His use of the English language is apparently much more colourful than that.'

'But there's a positive right there,' I said.

'There is?'

'Course there is. She's a girl but she's going to get her way on this. Good for her.'

'Well, sort of. She can't at this stage just turn up and join the year 11s; she'd be all at sea. So we've been in touch with the examining boards and it seems she's fine to sit the exams here, and in the run-up, to help her, we thought you could have her.'

'But what about the syllabus? How can she get through all that in three months?'

'Oh, she's already onto that – with that tutor I mentioned. Like I said, she's bright. Very able. And highly motivated, too. It'll be more exam preparation at this stage than anything, going over old papers and so on. We're showing willing, in essence. It's obviously important that we're seen to do that. Always got to keep OFSTED in mind, eh? Anyway, we can provide her with plenty of past papers, which she can practise on while she's with you.'

'As opposed to going into *any* regular classes?'

'Mr Giles is keen that she doesn't – doesn't want her mixing too much with boys, especially ones that aren't travellers – so this seems like the most workable option. Mike says she seems a nice girl. Outgoing. Friendly. Sounds like she could even be an asset to you with the younger ones. Anyway, Mr Giles is rather keen that you meet up with him to discuss things beforehand, so he can explain to you how he wants it all to work.'

I smiled at this role reversal. This would be nothing if not a novelty. 'I can understand that,' I said. 'It'll be useful for me as well. Tell him I'll see him any time it's convenient for him during the school day. Or just after, if that's easier. Granny too, if she likes.'

'Ah,' Gary said. 'Did I forget to mention that he doesn't do phones, and he doesn't do school visits?'

'But –'

'This morning excepted. Exceptional circumstances, apparently. I get the feeling there's been some jockeying for positon vis-à-vis his daughter. What he'd really like is for you to visit him on his site one day this week.'

'*Really*?' So, in effect, a summons. Now this *was* novel.

'Yes, any day as long as it's after four o'clock, apparently. The large blue and white caravan – you can't miss it apparently – second right. Two gilt lions at the bottom of the steps. I *think* that's right. Or was it *right*?'

Right, left, up, down – he was clearly finding this funny. 'Oh, Gary!' I said. '*Really*? Me go on a school visit to the traveller site?'

'I could come with you, if you like,' Gary said. 'In fact, thinking about it, perhaps I should.'

I didn't need to think about it at all. I could imagine Mike's face – as in my own Mike, as opposed to the head-teacher. Me go there? All five foot of me? Solo? 'Yes, please,' I said. 'I think I'd feel more relaxed if I had a minder. Not that I *need* one. Just that, well, you know …'

'Deal. Now how about a Bourbon?' Gary suggested, proffering a half pack of biscuits. 'Sort of by way of apology.'

'Bourbon, period, might be better,' I said, taking one anyway. 'Why does the phrase "The condemned man ate a hearty breakfast" spring so immediately to mind?'

'I have absolutely no idea at all,' Gary said. He pushed the pack under my nose again. 'But go ahead. Feel free to have two.'

Chapter 10

There's a phrase I rather like called 'dynamic equilibrium'. Goodness knows where I picked it up, because a scientist I am not, but it's a phrase Mr Hunt and his science department colleagues would know all about because it was normally used in chemistry to describe a state of balance that's achieved when all the things pulling in different directions were pulling at roughly the same rate.

It was a bit like that in the Unit at times, and thank goodness for that. If one child was acting up, it was usually the case that it was manageable because another was being uncharacteristically good. Or we'd get a new particularly challenging child come and join the Unit just as the last particularly challenging child left. It had been thankfully rare (well, so far, anyway) to have multiple crises, and though there seemed no rational explanation why this should be so, Kelly and I were both glad that it was.

It was a little like that now, in fact, with the summer term well under way; some children beginning to thrive, while others not so much. Jonathan, I was beginning to realise, was a very deeply unhappy boy. I knew his foster family were working hard to change things for him – he would tell me every day about how life was at home – but rather than make him realise that life should and *could* be better, it seemed only to make him resent his new family for being able to give him things his own family couldn't.

Poor, poor Jonathan. Instinct told me that was because he felt guilty; as though he was being disloyal to his flesh and blood family if he allowed himself to settle into his new life, and to enjoy aspects of it, which of course, impacted on his mood, and on his behaviour at school. It was as if he was determined to be naughty so that people wouldn't like him and was extremely upsetting to watch, when it played out. I could only hope that sometime soon he would let his new family in – let them give him the love he so desperately needed.

Tommy was a more straightforward character; one with a deep-seated dislike of and anger towards his stepfather – all of it justified – and a fierce, fierce loyalty towards his mother. It was part of what made him such a likeable little character, and also what made him emotionally robust, but he'd seen too much, done too much, suffered way too much trauma (both emotional and physical), and the way it played out for *him* – via that temper, that lashing out – meant we still had a bit of a way to go.

Chloe, on the other hand, was coming along in leaps and bounds. I had taken to sorting out her hair for her every morning, before the day got under way, and this small thing seemed to give her the protective shield she needed, and she was beginning to understand that her fellow pupils needed their personal space. And though I wondered how she'd fare once she was no longer in education, nothing had changed in my feeling that in the right environment – a specialist school, geared to meet her needs – there was no reason why she shouldn't reach her potential. I did wonder though what would happen when she was no longer with me.

Then there was Kiara, who continued to confound me. That first Monday when she'd been absent had turned out not to be a one-off. She'd been absent the following Monday, too.

'So you were ill again, love?' I'd asked her when she'd reappeared on the Tuesday morning, her father having called in the previous day – just as it had turned out he'd done the first week – to say she wouldn't be in as she'd been suffering from a stomach bug again.

'Bad tummy,' she confirmed. 'I think I ate too much rubbish over the weekend, miss. My dad's not a very good cook.'

I wondered if she'd simply latched onto a handy excuse. Our own head was currently off – which was unheard of – with a bad stomach. Did she think that would be the *excuse du jour*; that we might assume she had whatever he seemed to?

But what I mostly latched onto was her admission of where she'd been. 'You were staying at your dad's then?' I asked her. 'Staying over?'

This surprised me. The impression I'd been given was that a sleep-over with dad would be a no-no; that Kiara's mother wouldn't trust her ex to look after a hamster.

She nodded. 'Yeah, she lets me now,' she said, 'because she works so much at weekends. Silly me being at home on my own when he's just round the corner, isn't it? Saves her having to worry about what I'm up to,' she added. 'And being bored. When I'm with dad we have fun.'

'I'm sure you do,' I said, wondering at this change in arrangements. 'Though perhaps he could do with some cooking lessons?'

'Oh, he doesn't cook. He hasn't really got anything to cook with. We usually get take-aways delivered,' she added chattily. 'He reckons I must have had a dodgy kebab.'

But for all her poorly tummy, her eyes shone with happiness.

'I think I should pay him a visit,' I told Gary Clark the third Tuesday lunchtime, after another Monday when Kiara had failed to appear, even though our cast-iron head had been back for a fortnight. There'd been a voicemail left again, and, once again, he'd simply said she'd been feeling poorly. 'Don't you?' I said. 'I mean, that's three out of three Mondays she's missed now, isn't it?'

Gary nodded. 'Though the fact that he always calls reflects well on him, at least. And it might well be that she's swinging the lead with him, mightn't it? So she can stay longer with him, rather than go home to her mum. Have you tackled her about it?'

'I did this morning,' I confirmed, Gary's thoughts echoing my own. She wouldn't have been the first child in the universe keen to extend the weekend by feigning some sort of illness, and, given the circumstances, her dad might well be something of a soft touch. I was beginning to feel a little sorry for Mr Bentley, as I was sure Kiara could wind anyone round her little finger if she had a mind to. 'She said the same as she did last week – that she must have eaten something funny.'

'And you don't believe her.'

I shook my head. 'No. No, not for a minute. I think you're right. I think it's either that she's pulling the wool over his eyes because she likes staying with him, or that he's complicit – given his background, he might not have much inclination to lay down the law and insist that she goes to school. Or doesn't have an alarm clock. There's always that.'

Gary nodded. 'Or he likes having her around running errands for him. It's been known. From the little we do know, a sense of responsibility doesn't seem to be his strong point.'

'I agree,' I said. 'Not that I want to pre-judge him. There's no doubt Kiara's happier as a result of spending time with him. And perhaps – well, if he's going to play a bigger part in her life, anyway – he just needs a bit of guidance.' I smiled. 'At the very least so he's clear that sending Kiara to school isn't a lifestyle choice but a legal requirement.'

'And you want to be the one to put him straight on that, I'm guessing. I'll get hold of a phone number for you, and if no luck, we'll send a note home. D'you want me to go with you?'

'D'you want to check if he has a dog first this time?' I quipped.

Though I really didn't mean to laugh quite so loud.

We'd yet to have Morgan, the girl from the travelling family, physically join us – she was due to start with me straight after half-term – but, as per her father's directive a couple of weeks previously, I'd already been to see her the previous week. And it had been something of an eye opener, too – in more ways than one.

Gary and I had set off straight after school that same Thursday, taking his car, rather than mine, so that I could do the navigating. Though both of us knew the big Groves estate we'd need to go through to get to the traveller site, neither of us knew it well enough to be confident about the complicated instructions we'd been given. It was a huge, sprawling estate, right on the edge of town and backing onto countryside and, once we were through it, assuming we'd found the right exit from it, we found ourselves driving gingerly along a long dirt road in the sunshine, our route flanked by the nodding heads of cow parsley and the last few bits of hawthorn blossom, and punctuated by enormous pot-holes. It seemed to go on for ever; at least a good couple of miles, right into what felt like the middle of nowhere, only wide enough for one car and with the odd bulge for passing. Luckily, we didn't meet anyone coming the other way.

'No danger of any local residents kicking off, at least,' Gary observed, reading my thoughts as the track grew ever narrower, and the hedgerows began to be replaced by ranks of trees, their canopies of leaves now plunging us into deep shade. 'Getting a bit spooky down here, isn't it?'

I agreed with him, mightily glad I'd not come here on my own. Not that I intended admitting that. 'Oh, you big wuss!' I joked. Then, 'Oh, look! I think we're here. I can see a pair of gates ahead. Big gates – wasn't that what he said?'

Gary slowed the car down and as we drew nearer, it seemed we were indeed there. We had to be – there was nowhere else to go. I was just about to say so when I almost jumped out of my car seat, if not my skin, as two enormous Alsatian dogs seemed to appear out of nowhere, leaping – no, more lunging – towards us, teeth bared.

'Shit!' squeaked Gary. 'What the …?'

I was too scared to speak. It was only when I realised they were both on chains – one was attached to either gate-post – that I could gulp in air to breathe. Yes, we were in a car, but we both had our windows fully open – a teacher's salary (even a teacher with a gold plaque on his office door) not generally lending itself to posh air-conditioned cars.

'God,' Gary said with feeling, as he made a lunge himself, for the 'up' window button. 'Bloody things scared the life out of me! Thanks, Mr Giles,' he muttered. 'Brilliant directions. And you might have bothered to mention the two enormous bloody dogs!'

I was too nervous myself now to laugh at Gary's obvious terror, and not knowing what to do, quite, we sat in the car and waited, while the dogs, straining at their chains, barked at the car.

We didn't wait long. It would have been a miracle if anyone within half a mile hadn't heard them, after all. And, sure enough, a huge hulk of a man with olive skin and with jet black hair appeared. He stared out over the gates at us – they were just under his head-height – then began undoing what I presumed was a giant bolt on the other side of the gates. 'Park your car in that layby,' he shouted above the dogs' din. 'Ya can't bring that thing in here. Who is it yer wanting anyway?'

I glanced at Gary, who had wasted no time in slamming the car into reverse, as if he was starring in a cop movie. Which seemed a bit overly dramatic.

'Granny and Mr Giles,' I shouted back from my still-open window. 'They're expecting us.'

'Get on with it, then,' he yelled, as he began swinging one of the gates open. 'Now hurry up before these dogs go fekking mad.'

It was a funny accent he had, I thought. Not quite Irish, but there was definitely a twang there; it was an accent I didn't think I'd come across before. I helped Gary with instructions as he reversed the car back down the narrow track to the last passing space, and wondered it was something unique to different groups of travellers. As they kept themselves largely to themselves, it would stand to reason that something unique to them might have emerged.

Gary killed the engine and as I reached over to the back seat to grab my satchel, I realised that his hands were still gripping the wheel.

'Are you okay?' I asked, noticing that his face was pale as well now. 'What's wrong?'

He turned to face me. 'Look, would you mind going in without me?' he asked. 'Only I'm not sure I'm going to be able to get past those dogs.'

'They're chained up.'

'Yes, but on long chains.'

'Yes, but I'm sure that man over there will take hold of them or something. He's not going to just let them take chunks out of us, is he?'

I said it with more confidence than I actually felt, but, no, that was being silly. Of course he'd hold on to them. The last thing he'd want was a dangerous dogs charge against him. And what was I even *thinking*? Once they knew we weren't trespassing – that we'd been given the okay – they'd probably leap up and lick us to death.

'No, it's not that,' Gary explained, looking more traumatised than I think I'd ever seen him. 'I really don't think I'm going to be *able* to get past them. I have a phobia of dogs, Casey. I'm sorry – I should have thought, shouldn't I? You're right, I *am* a wuss. Sorry – why didn't I *think*?'

It was obvious, too. It wasn't *that* warm, yet his forehead was clammy. And he looked like he was on the verge of having a panic attack. Which we couldn't have happen, out here, in the middle of nowhere.

'No problem,' I reassured him. 'God, Gary, why *didn't* you think? I could have brought Jim along. Or Kelly. She'd probably eat those brutes for breakfast, wouldn't she?' I was rewarded with a nod. 'Look, are you *sure* you'll be okay? Do my window up for starters.' I rummaged in my bag. 'And here's half a bottle of water. I'll be as quick as I can. And if I'm not back in half an hour, call the cavalry!'

Who knew? I thought, as I strode back to the gates – one now fully open – to find our burly host had indeed taken the brace of dogs in hand. Both were now panting, tails wagging, tongues lolling from the sides of their mouths. I stuck a hand out. 'I'm Casey Watson from the school,' I said, 'And you are?'

The man wiped his free hand across the back of his jeans and roughly shook mine. 'They call me Daniel. Daniel Shay. I'll take you across to Paddy's van now.'

He then pulled the gate to behind us, leaving the dogs back outside, where they immediately ran to the ends of their chains, and took up what was at least a now silent vigil scaring the bejesus out of poor Gary.

Daniel Shay led me through the site and I took in my surroundings. There were around 12 caravans, all arranged in a kind of rough semi-circle, some with little patches of neatly tended garden to the front of them, and some with awnings erected which seemed to serve as outdoor kitchen/ dining areas. I could hear a stream running somewhere, and as I looked around, I noticed another area festooned with rows of laundry lines, some with clothes drying, and a building block that I guessed housed toilets or showers.

It was dog central, and I was glad Gary had stayed put in the car. There seemed to be a dog or two stationed outside almost every van, though none took more than a passing, and benign, interest as we passed them. The huge area we were walking across seemed to be filled with young children too, running around, semi-naked, or playing. One or two glanced at me but none seemed particularly interested either.

I spotted the Giles's caravan right away. There were indeed lions guarding it and it was indeed blue and white. A cheerful blue, too. It was immaculate.

'Granny and Paddy's van, ma'am,' Daniel said as he pointed. 'They'll see you coming, so there's no need to knock.' He left me then, and strode back across the site to where he'd come from, while I stared up at the windows and wondered what to do. True to Daniel's words, I didn't wonder for too long. Only a couple of moments later another giant of a man appeared, looking far too big to fit into a caravan.

'Mrs Watson, is it?' he called to me. 'Away in, come on.' He stepped back inside so that I could pass him. I edged inside to find an old lady sitting on a sofa – Granny Giles, I presumed. I smiled and said hello.

'Sit yerself down,' Mr Giles insisted, pointing towards an armchair. 'My Morgan will be along in a minute to make us all some tea.'

I duly sat and looked around, somewhat dumbstruck. I didn't know what I was expecting, as I'd never been inside a traveller's caravan before, but this was just exquisite. A beautiful, spotless three-piece suite set on a carpet that was so pale it was almost white. Expensive-looking curtains that I was sure would have had to be custom-made. The kitchen I'd passed was just as beautiful; like something out of a high-end kitchen showroom, and the display cabinet that divided the two parts of the living area, was filled with delicate porcelain ornaments that were charming and reminded me of my childhood.

'Admiring me china?' the old lady said, her voice gravelly and give-away deep. She had obviously smoked heavily for many years.

'Oh yes,' I said, and meant it, as I'd recognised it immediately as probably being by one of the most famous Italian porcelain manufacturers of them all. I knew because my mum used to collect it while I was growing up, and make me dust it for her. Not a quick job at all. I was stunned to see so much of it in this one bijou caravan. 'They're beautiful. Is it all Capodimonte?' I asked her.

'Aye, it is,' she said smiling broadly, as if I'd just passed some important test. 'And rare pieces most of them, too. Cost an arm and a leg to replace them, it would.' She glanced across proudly at her son. 'My Patrick buys me a piece every birthday and Christmas.'

Mr Giles laughed at this, almost making the air vibrate. 'Jesus, mother! If I had done that you'd surely have fekking hundreds of the bloody things!'

Granny Giles laughed as well, a warm, guttural, belly laugh, and I had rush of a warm feeling about this family. Just then a young boy of about seven burst through the door, making me fear for the delicate porcelain only inches from me. Did they blue-tack it all down I wondered? I would have.

The little boy – who looked to be around seven or eight, was wearing only a pair of shorts and had nothing on his feet. He was jumping about and had one hand firmly clutching the front of his shorts. 'Oh, Granny, I need a piss,' he said, in that same, slightly Irish accent. 'Please let me use your lavvy, Granny, *please*, just this once.'

The old lady picked up an ornate walking stick from beside her seat and shook it at the lad. 'How many times, boy? How many times do I hear your da' shouting you in for a piss? Go on then, but it's the last time, you hear? Or I'll take my fekking stick to you.'

The boy grinned widely. 'Thank you, Granny. Love you!' he added, then quickly opened a door and disappeared through it.

I was confused. 'Is that your grandson, too?' I asked, wondering about the many children I'd seen here. Were some of them at the local primary? Who was educating them?

'Not at all!' she said. 'But I'm Granny to one and all around here. It's the way things are, is all. I'm 88, you know,' she added, in that proud way elderly ladies did everywhere. 'So I've earned me respect. Don't barely have to lift a finger these days, I don't.'

Neither did Mr Giles, it seemed, because Morgan herself joined us, moments later, and once the little boy had been shooed out, she greeted me demurely, then set about making tea, taking down bone-china cups and saucers and providing a plate of biscuits – no grabbing one out of the packet, like we did in school.

She was a lovely looking girl – more a young woman than a girl, actually – with her father's dark eyes and the same full head of wavy hair. I was looking forward to learning more about her. Though that wouldn't be happening today, it transpired, as no sooner had she put the tea down in front of her grandmother than she was shooed away herself, which, again – presumably because she'd won the battle to get herself installed at school and take her GCSEs – she seemed happy enough to do, while Mr Giles told me how it would be.

And how it would be meant extracting a number of promises. That I'd keep a close eye on her; that she wouldn't be 'running around, mixing with "gorgers"' (which I later learned meant countrymen or non-gypsy); that though Mr Giles wasn't pleased that she was doing exams in the first place, I'd make good and sure when she was with me that she didn't waste her time, so that when she took them she'd 'fekking pass them, as well!'

Then, having been able to reassure him on all points – as well as Granny, obviously – I was able to trot back with Mr Giles, out of the gate, to the layby in the lane – the dogs now strangely absent – where I half expected to find Gary sitting there either mauled to death or blowing into a paper bag.

'I think I've just been sized up,' I told him, once I'd checked his vital signs and found them fine. 'Seriously.'

Just like I was now hopefully going to be doing with Kiara's dad. Though I doubted he had much Capodimonte.

Chapter 11

Gary had had little difficulty tracking down Mr Bentley's number – Kiara had his mobile listed as one of her emergency contacts when they had been routinely updated the previous term. It had then just been a case of my leaving a message on his voicemail, which was responded to within less than an hour of my leaving it. Yes, of course he'd be happy to meet me – Kiara had already told him all about me – and yes, of course, it would be fine for me to come and visit him at home, though he'd be more than happy to come into school, if that was easier. He'd also warned me that, while he was okay with me coming to him, he didn't 'live in a palace'.

Speaking to Mr Bentley on the phone told me little other than he seemed a quiet, possibly shy man – he'd sounded nervous, yes, but not excessively so. He'd been reasonably articulate, perfectly polite – what sort of a job might he have had before becoming long-term unemployed, I wondered? – and not remotely obstructive or defensive, all of which seemed to bode well.

Knowing what I already did about the family dynamic, it was hard not to form an impression in advance of what I might find when I met him in person. That he was held in pretty low regard by his ex wasn't in question. That there was long-standing acrimony was something I'd learned early on, and there was nothing unusual about that.

I'd even learned that he was a 'waste of space' – that had been one of the first things Kiara's mum had told me about him, and it stuck. Living in squalor, unemployed, reliant on benefits – it wasn't the most encouraging CV out there.

But I was prepared to be open-minded because that was the only way to be; there were two sides to every story, after all. Yes, Kiara's mum might look down on him, but her domestic standards were right up there with my own and, from what I'd seen when I'd visited, she had a similar cleaning obsession. Even worse, perhaps; at least I allowed my kids to make a mess before bustling round to clear it all up.

There was also the inescapable fact that whenever Kiara spoke about her dad, there was a real light of love in her eyes, and that she enjoyed spending time with him wasn't in question. Which reminded me that good parenting went on all over the planet, often by adults who struggled in many other aspects of life, but found maternal or paternal love the easiest thing in the world.

I also knew how fiercely loyal Kiara was to her father. So much so that I got the impression that she'd fight his corner over pretty much anything; and perhaps that, too, was the result of the acrimonious nature of the relationship between her parents. With her mother so down on him, she felt she had to stand up for him.

And perhaps that was because he was genuinely trying to do his best. Yes, he might have been absent for a chunk of her childhood, but perhaps now he was trying to make good the lack – perhaps he was trying to be a genuinely good dad to her. And that was surely a major new positive in her life; something to be cherished and encouraged. It just needed to be tempered by some good old-fashioned guidance about the importance, when she was with him, of making sure she attended school.

Such was my mindset as I parked the car and locked it the following Wednesday afternoon; that I was there to help make Kiara's dad see where his responsibilities lay and help him to help us in helping her. He didn't actually live very far from Kiara and her mother, as the crow flies, but the distance travelled, in terms of affluence, was far. Mr Bentley lived in a part of town I was already quite familiar with: a mix of elderly people, who'd lived there for most of their lives, living side by side with flat dwellers, these being the sort of houses that, over the years, had been bought up by developers and converted into apartments for the rental market. It was therefore a previously grand street, now down at heel, and with only a precarious sense of community – one that could all too easily be crumbled by a single all-night party, or altercation about parking or bins.

I had lived in such environments and knew what a melting pot they were, and as I climbed out of the car, I tried not to see the negatives that seemed to shout out from my immediate surroundings. The abandoned mattress half slumped again a wall on the opposite pavement, the broken glass (legacy of a thousand abandoned beer bottles?), the graffiti'd brickwork, the bits of rubbish that were light enough to be picked up by the breeze wafting in idle swirls along the street.

Try as I might, however, I still felt like a duck in a shooting gallery as I crossed the road to the house I'd identified as the correct one; the run-down Victorian terrace being indistinguishable from most of the others in the street, which had presumably been converted into three or four separate flats.

There were three buzzers, in fact, when I fetched up at the porch, which was separated from the pavement by no more than four or five feet of 'garden'; in reality enough space for a quartet of council wheelie bins and a healthy profusion of weeds. The panel of buzzers was sufficiently faded that the names written to accompany them had all but vanished, but the number scrawled in marker pen led me to the correct one. The top one, so presumably the top flat.

I pressed the buzzer and the speaker crackled into life immediately, whereupon a soft male voice said hello, the same one I'd heard on the phone.

'I'm Casey Watson,' I explained, wondering if he'd watched my arrival. 'From the school? Here to have a chat with you about Kiara?'

'I'll come down,' came the reply. 'The entry buzzer's broken. Hang on a tick …'

The speaker went dead then, but within seconds I heard a rumble from inside that was unmistakably the sound of someone clattering down the stairs. The door was then opened, with the rattle of a security chain and a squeal of protesting hinges, presumably long starved of grease.

The same could not be said for Mr Bentley. He couldn't have looked more different from Kiara's mother, his sex notwithstanding. Where she was pin-sharp and straight-backed, he was sloppiness personified; there was no part of him that suggested he had any sort of grooming regime, bar getting out of bed and raking hands through his hair.

'Good afternoon,' I said, automatically holding a hand out to shake and then trying to push away the thought that sprang to mind as he looked at it, namely: 'Shaggy from *Scooby Doo*! That's who he looks like!'

Mr Bentley put his own hand in it, and his handshake was surprisingly firm. And, despite the look of him – elderly jeans, frayed T-shirt, greasy shoulder-length hair – his smile was welcoming and his manner engaging. 'Come on up,' he said. 'Follow me. I've already put the kettle on.'

I duly did so, skirting round the piles of junk mail that formed a drift against the hall skirting board, and placing my feet, as did he, in the centre of the stair treads, which were darkened in colour on either side by what looked like a year's worth of dust; clearly no one took responsibility for cleaning the 'common parts' here. I doubted anyone in residence owned a vacuum cleaner.

My impression – that Mr Bentley lived in what would once have been called a 'hovel' – didn't change on entering the flat itself. It was as filthy as Kiara's mum's home had been clean, as poorly furnished as hers had been fitted out like a show home. He led me down a short hallway – carpet coloured as on the staircase, a kind of 'greige', striped with 'dust' – into a back room that obviously served as kitchen-diner. As we drew nearer, I could see out onto a small balcony atop a fire escape, which presumably led down to a back garden. There was a single black refuse sack sitting squat like a beanbag by the glass-panelled back door, perhaps evidence of a hasty tidy up.

'Tea or coffee?' Mr Bentley said brightly, brandishing two blue mugs. Spying that the jar on the counter wasn't some icky bargain-priced coffee 'blend', I opted for the latter. As a fully paid-up member of the coffee-addict community, I took great interest on where I got my fixes.

'Black,' I added, noting that despite the down-at-heel nature of my immediate surroundings the surfaces were freshly wiped, at least. There was a small formica-topped table and I wondered if this was where he and Kiara sat and ate their take-aways. 'And thanks for agreeing to see me,' I said, matching his chatty tone – at least here I didn't feel I was on pins. 'Kiara tells me you've not long moved back to the area, and that she's really been enjoying spending time with you.'

Mr Bentley had his back to me, spooning coffee into mugs, but now he turned and nodded. 'Only six months or so,' he said. 'I'm, um, trying to find some work. I used to work in haulage, and it's, well –' He shrugged. 'Work's hard to come by everywhere, isn't it? Sorry,' he added, casting around the room as he spoke. 'You know, for the state of the place. The mess and that … it's not that easy to make ends meet some weeks …'

I realised then that, despite his chirpy smile, he was actually quite nervous. Intimidated by me, even, which was novel. But seen from his perspective, perhaps I did cut an intimidating figure; smartly turned out, business-like, sent from Kiara's school. I doubted that, in his current circumstances, he got lots of visitors like me – only had dealings with them at the job centre, in council offices and so on, where I didn't doubt he'd be routinely judged. I felt sorry for him suddenly, and keen to put him at his ease. Which meant moving things along to Kiara.

'Oh, believe me, I've been there,' I reassured him, putting my bag down on the little table, noticing as I did so that there was a piece of paper with a shopping list on it, written in Kiara's hand. 'I'm not here to pass judgement on your soft furnishings,' I added grinning. 'Just keen to chat about Kiara. She speaks very highly of you in school.'

'That's nice,' he said, and again I thought of Shaggy – he gave the impression of being something like a gauche teenager in a thirty-something male's body, and I couldn't imagine him and Kiara's mum together at *all*.

The coffee soon made – true to his word, he obviously had already boiled the kettle – he then ushered me into a second, bigger room at the front, allowing me a brief covert glimpse into one of the bedrooms, which seemed to sport little more than a cheap-looking divan bed (unmade) and one of those hanging rails you can buy to hang up extra clothes. The bedside table was an upturned plastic storage box.

The living room fared little better. There was a sagging sofa, a matching chair and a low wooden coffee table, which boasted so many cup rings it looked like an Olympic-themed art installation. *Oh*, I couldn't help but think, as Mr Bentley placed our mugs on it, *what I could do for that with some vinegar, some wood stain and a big tub of wax.* For all that, though, the room felt a million times more homely than Mrs Bentley's gleaming kitchen, not least because evidence of human occupation was all around me, and, more specifically, evidence that Kiara spent time here. As well as a photo-montage of her propped up on a battered cupboard in the corner, there were teenage girl-mags, obviously well thumbed, a pair of girly pink slippers and, in the centre of the coffee table, a bottle of nail varnish and a hair-bobble sat beside the TV remote.

I took the sofa, he took the chair and I picked up my coffee. It would be too hot to drink for at least ten long minutes, but I sipped on it anyway, conscious that there were few things more awkward than being done with whatever you'd gone to a place to do, and still having half a mug of steaming coffee to finish up.

'So,' I said, 'first off, I do need to ask you about Kiara having missed three Mondays in a row. What do you make of that? Does she often complain of tummy problems when she's with you?'

He hesitated, and I could see that this questioning was making him uncomfortable so I decided to use a different angle. 'Mr Bentley, trust me, I know how girls of Kiara's age can be at times. I have a daughter myself and I well remember that if she was desperate for a day off, rather than come to me, she would go to her dad and use the "tummy pain" excuse. They're not daft, girls – they know that most men get a little squeamish about such things.' I laughed then, and Mr Bentley nodded what looked like an admission that he'd been duped exactly like that.

'Guilty as charged, probably,' he agreed, picking up his mug.

There seemed little point in pursuing that line – I'd proffered a possible reason and he'd taken it – and my hunch was that when it came to Kiara he was as soft as he looked. Perhaps next Monday, however, he'd toughen up a little. And if not, well, then it would be time to become more pointed.

I was much more interested in Kiara's issues, in any case. So I asked him what he thought might be the cause of her chronic tiredness, the hair pulling, the seeming lack of friends – but it seemed he had little to offer.

'I honestly don't know,' he said. 'She's fine when she's with me. We have *fun*. We go out, we stay in, we go shopping. She's *fine*. She never pulls her hair and she never says anything about being unhappy – well, except what you'd expect her to – that she's not very happy living with her mum.'

I was about to respond, to try and draw him on that particular dynamic, when he answered the question without me having to. 'Look,' he said, 'I know she's bound to say that – of course she is. I'm not stupid. But she's got a point, hasn't she? Spending all that time home alone when she could be here with me. It's not like I haven't got room for her. And can you blame her? Her mother out till all hours, no dinner, no one to put her to bed. It's not right, is it?' He spread his palms as if to entreat me to agree with him. 'I know I've not got much –' He smiled ruefully as he said this. 'Though I'm working on that one, honest. But, come on,' he finished, reaching for his mug again and draining it, 'it's not right her being there.'

I sensed a shift in Kiara's dad's tone as he said this, and recalled Kiara telling me how, as soon as she was old enough, she was leaving her mum's and going to live with her father. Perhaps this was something they'd discussed at length. Perhaps this was key. Perhaps Mr Bentley was making plans to try and help grant Kiara's wishes – to have her live with him full time right now.

But would Mrs Bentley ever allow that? I didn't think so. Though she wasn't helping herself if she was still working several nights a week leaving Kiara without a responsible adult. 'We *are* concerned about the hours Kiara's mum is working,' I agreed. 'But at the same time, we do understand that it's hard; she needs to earn a living, and if she works in a job with unsociable hours, well, it's difficult, isn't it?'

I wondered if Mr Bentley would take that as a criticism of him, but it seemed to be water off a duck's back. 'Which is why she should allow Kiara to stay here more often,' he said. 'Look, I know I've been a bit soft on her, but that'll stop, I promise –'

'Mr Bentley, it's not up to the school to dictate your living arrangements,' I hurried to point out. 'We're just keen to ensure that Kiara is in the best place – emotionally, that is – to thrive and reach her potential, and our main concern currently is what appears to be a difficult situation between you and her mother; that ...' I paused, trying to choose my words, '... that the animosity between you and Mrs Bentley is taking its toll, on both her physical and psychological health.'

I drank some more coffee while Mr Bentley took this in. 'I don't know what to say to you,' he said eventually, drawing his hand through his hair to get it out of his eyes. It was longer than Mrs Bentley's and I wondered if the bobble belonged to him. 'I really don't. I don't know what she's been saying to you, but you've said yourself that she's out all bloody hours. Working her "unsociable hours".' He seemed to think for a bit then looked directly at me, pointedly. 'I suppose she told you she's a carer?'

'Yes,' I said. 'Well, that she works in a care home, anyway. She didn't specify in what capacity. But, yes.'

He nodded, as if satisfied that I'd answered correctly. 'Well, let me tell you, you're right. She cares, all right,' he said. 'Takes care of all the blokes that are willing to pay her a tenner for a quickie down some alley. You know what I'm saying?' He paused to smile mirthlessly. 'You beginning to get my drift?'

Chapter 12

Still in shock, I decided to drive straight back to school to see if I could catch someone before they left for home. This really wasn't something I wanted to sit on all night. I was hopeful, as well, because almost all of the teaching staff, and certainly Gary, tended to stay on for at least an hour and often more at the end of the school day, there being scant time available, even with many of us starting an hour early, to prepare everything that needed preparing ready for the following school day.

I hadn't stayed long after Mr Bentley's revelation. It had been altogether too much to take in. And he'd point blank refused to be drawn further into it. Though he didn't seem to be regretting spilling the beans regarding his ex-wife's *real* profession (about which I was gobsmacked – could that really be true?) he would not comment further except to repeat what he'd already said: 'You know what I'm saying?' Well, yes, shocking as it was, I did.

I'd asked to use the facilities, however, grim though I'd imagined they'd be to someone with a bleach habit as entrenched as I had, and on the way back (reasonably untraumatised, when compared with what he'd just told me) I took the opportunity to poke my head round the door to the second bedroom, which looked pretty much the same as the other rooms I'd been in – bar a newly painted pink wall, that was – *check*. Though Kiara was obviously expected to sleep on a mattress on the floor, amid half a dozen of those checked, woven zip-up plastic laundry bags, which I presumed formed the remainder of Mr Bentley's storage.

When I returned to the living room, Mr Bentley himself had been bustling around, tidying up further – almost as if he expected his revelation to set a ball rolling, and that he wanted the place looking nice before the next 'official' came round. I really didn't know what to make of any of it.

I was therefore now desperate to speak to Gary. Yes, it could have waited – what difference was a day going to make, after all? But I didn't want to wait. I just couldn't get to grips with what Mr Bentley had told me and I needed to share it with someone else. It just sounded like the most unlikely thing imaginable, even though, at the same time, my brain was now working overtime, remembering all the oddities and inconsistencies in what I'd already seen and heard, and trying to overlay what I knew of Kiara's life with her mother, with what I'd just seen of her father. Most of all, I needed guidance about how best I should follow it up – and I was keen to get some before I saw Kiara the following morning, because I knew that *what* I knew would affect everything.

I was in luck. I could hear Gary tapping away on his keyboard even as I headed down the corridor. Still there, then. I knocked on the open door as I went in.

'You heard, then?' he asked me. 'Poor Mike.'

'Poor Mike what?' I asked him. '*Which* Mike?'

'Sorry,' he said. '*Our* Mike. Looks like he's going to have to have his appendix out after all.'

'After all?' I asked, taking the seat he'd gestured I sit down on.

'Sorry – you're probably not up to speed. That's what it's been – a "grumbling" appendix. Grumbling no more, apparently. Full on complaining. He left in an ambulance, just over an hour back – you might have even passed it on your way to your visit.'

'Oh, my God – is he alright?'

'Well, no one seemed to think that he wouldn't be, least of all him,' he said. 'You know what his last words were when we waved him off to hospital?'

'No. What?'

'They'll think I've rigged it – just so we can postpone the inspection!'

Gary laughed. 'Respect, eh? And, of course, he's right. They'll probably have to.'

'Oh my goodness,' I said again. 'I hadn't thought of that.'

'So that's not why you're here then,' Gary said.

'No, no, it's not,' I said, mentally regrouping.

'I know that face, Casey,' Gary said. 'What's wrong?'

'There's been a development,' I told him as I sat down. 'With Mr Bentley.'

Gary clicked his mouse and put his computer to sleep temporarily. 'Okayyy ... What sort of development? "Not an encouraging one" would be my educated guess.'

'It would be a good guess as well,' I said. 'I'm shell-shocked, to be honest. Though it's not about him. It's about what he's *told* me.'

'Which is?'

I relayed the gist of my meeting with Kiara's father and, as verbatim as I could, what he'd said to me before I left, watching Gary's reactions to it as I spoke. I had been horrified myself, perhaps even more gobsmacked than I might have been, because if it was all true, it wasn't just that Mrs Bentley didn't look like a prostitute: if it really was, then I'd been completely and utterly hoodwinked. But perhaps that was my failing, for having such a clear idea in my head of what a prostitute would look like. Which was insane anyway. I knew as much as the next person about Cynthia Payne, didn't I? Which was a thought that really brought me up short.

But Gary never so much as raised an eyebrow, much less flinched. 'Ri-ight,' he said finally, once I'd finished recounting the details. 'So.'

He left a pause, as if to collect his thoughts, but more, I thought, from habit. His was a job that required an element of calm and cool rather than a tendency to hot-headedness, however hair-raising some of the things he'd seen and heard. 'We-ell,' he went on finally, 'the first thing we have to consider is that what you've been told could just be bitter tit-for-tat nonsense, couldn't it? We both know there is no love lost between the pair of them, after all. On the other hand, if it *is* true, then we have something else to consider.' Another pregnant pause. 'And that is – is it even our business?'

I was stunned. It was obviously my day for being stunned. 'What?' I said, aghast. 'But of course it's our business! How could it not be?'

Gary moved a pen a couple of inches across his desk. 'But, Casey, if Kiara is being looked after, fed, clothed and generally brought up well, then she isn't in any danger, is she? Yes, granted, what her mother *might* be doing to earn a living is against the law – and, if so, potentially actionable, but not necessarily by the school. Unless Kiara is at risk, then I have to be careful how I approach something like this. Yes, again, as a Child Protection Officer, I have a duty of care towards the child, but I also have to be *very* sure about the facts before throwing around any accusations. Imagine the implications. Kiara would be snatched up from that lovely home you saw, and taken into care, which would obviously be very traumatic for her, and also for ever smeared by the allegations against her mother. Do you see? We have to consider the possible consequences. We have to think.'

I didn't want to think at that moment. I wanted to act. But after allowing Gary's words to sink in, I realised he had a valid point. The last thing I wanted was to be the cause of turning Kiara's life upside down, particularly if all it came down to was a bunch of nasty, unfounded allegations by her ex.

'You're right.' I sighed. 'I know you're right. But oh, I'm so *angry*, Gary. If it turns out to be true, then that woman is some bloody actress, I'll give her that. It's making me wonder though, it really is. On the way back here, you know what struck me most? That every single time I've ever mentioned her mum's job, Kiara's given me this strange look – a weird sort of look, as though she knows something I don't. Do you know what I mean? Well, you probably don't – it's not even something I can really pin down – just this sense that there's something going on behind her eyes. Something that makes me think she's carrying around secrets. Perhaps that's key to everything; perhaps that's why she keeps herself to herself, doesn't have friends round the house ... God, Gary – d'you think Mrs Bentley takes *clients home*?'

'Whoah, there, 'Gary said. 'You're running away with yourself here, Casey. All we have is a derogatory comment by an obviously antagonistic ex. And with some motivation, given what you've told me about the situation. Perhaps it's all part of a ploy to get more access to his child. Though if so, slinging mud isn't exactly the best way to go about it –'

'But it might be *true*.'

'You could be right,' Gary conceded. 'But even so, it's important we don't act in haste. To be honest, this is something I'd like to talk through with Mike first, which – hmm, not the best timing, is it?' I shook my head. No, it wasn't.

'Which isn't going to be able to happen for a good bit now, I don't think. Which means I need to speak to someone else. Someone who can guide me through the protocol for a situation like this. If indeed there even *is* one.'

But I was still having visions of what sort of things – well, potentially at least – young Kiara might be being exposed to. No wonder she felt isolated. No wonder she wanted to be with her father. No wonder she was tired all the time and had developed a self-soothing tic. For me, it was all adding up now. 'Can't we speak to Donald?' I suggested. 'As deputy, wouldn't he be automatically the man to go to when the head's not here?'

Gary nodded. 'Indeed we could, and perhaps we should, but I'm still inclined to caution. He'd have said the same as me; that it would make sense to run things by Mike first – or someone in a position of similar authority, anyway. We also need to properly review the evidence we *do* have; perhaps even to talk more to Kiara herself. Not overtly. I think "softly softly" is the way to go here. At least in the short term. If she's not deemed at risk – which it doesn't appear she is, then we have to wait and sit it out, I'm afraid.' He leaned closer, as if to emphasis his next words. 'Though, trust me, Casey, I won't just leave this; I promise, I will do a bit of digging.'

I could only wait and hope, then – that he dug down deep enough.

Life is full of ironies, in all sorts of ways, and nothing seemed as ironic as the situation I found myself in over the following week. When I was told that Mr Moore wouldn't be returning till sometime after the half-term holidays (and he *had* had his appendix out, to be fair) I found myself in exactly the same situation as I imagined Kiara was in with *me* – possessed of a secret that I couldn't share with her. And just to heap a further irony upon the one I was already carrying, I'd never seen her so apparently happy. Strange and closed-off and self-contained as she had been up to now, I was beginning to see an alternative Kiara; more outgoing – she and Chloe were apparently very much BFFs – and more relaxed as well; she now seemed to be leaving her hair alone. And though I suspected she was still up far too late in the evenings, there was a spring in her step that I'd not seen before.

Her father's doing? When she skipped in the following Monday (he was good as his word, then) I wondered if her brightness was born out of the belief that he was going to arrange things so she could stay with him more. Or, more than that – would he even try for custody? Wouldn't any father, knowing what he knew?

But then, how did he know? And how *long* had he known? There was just so much we didn't know, and it grated on me. And there was a third irony, right there in front of me. Just as Kiara was sorting out her life and happiness, I was basically plotting to destroy it. It just didn't add up.

* * *

The half-term holiday seemed to take an age coming round, but at least I had something else to focus on: the fact that we'd be moving into our lovely new bungalow. And though it meant I'd spent every weeknight coming home from work and then lugging furniture and filling boxes, I couldn't have been happier about the timing.

There was also the fact that it meant I could go shopping. A new home naturally meant I needed new things to go in it – at the very least new curtains, new light shades, and new rugs and cushions. Everyone knew this. It was a family given.

'But why?' Mike moaned on the Saturday night when, with me surrounded by catalogues, he could hardly find a space on the sofa. 'It's only two bloody minutes since you changed everything last time! Why does every move come with spending a fortune?'

'You know the old saying,' I told him. 'Out with the old, in with the new. That's why.'

'Er, Mum,' Kieron butted in, 'I think that saying is supposed to be used on New Year's Eve – not every time anyone moves house.'

I gave my 'too clever for his own good' son a withering look. 'Even *so*,' I pointed out, 'you grotty pair probably won't have noticed, but all the old stuff is so out of date now, it's practically ancient. We're upgrading and that's that. I wouldn't *dare* hang these old curtains in that new neighbourhood!'

But, for all my excitement, the move itself didn't go quite as smoothly as I'd hoped. Having taken a week off at

Easter, Mike had been unable to do so again, and Kieron wasn't much help either. Yes, he'd got the week off from college, but had gone to play football as usual the first Saturday and had, rather conveniently to my mind, badly twisted his ankle.

With Kieron out of action, and Riley at work, I'd had no choice but to beg help from my poor beleaguered parents, who, though fit and pretty well, were both in their sixties and hadn't done much in the way of heavy lifting for quite a few years. As a result I had to do the bulk of it, which meant it all went very slowly, leading to the realisation that the sensible thing would be to take an extra day off at the end of half-term.

I was perfectly within my rights to do this, as it was part of my contract, but I still felt awful when I called the school early on the Monday morning, to explain that I wouldn't make it in till the Wednesday. I felt bad because it meant that Jim, my fellow behaviour manager, would have to take over the Unit for me, and worse still when the school secretary reminded me that Morgan, the traveller girl who was coming to sit her GCSEs, would be starting, and I wouldn't be there to welcome her myself.

Eventually, by the Tuesday evening – just in the nick of time – we were settled into my perfect bungalow, even sitting out on our new decking, tired, yes, but happy to be finally installed in our new home. And as I contemplated the graft we'd put in, and the bubble bath I'd be enjoying later, I realised I'd hardly thought about work in days. Which had to be a good thing, as it had really recharged my batteries. So much so that I realised I was looking forward to going back to school and getting stuck in to whatever came next. Which is probably why you should be careful what you wish for.

But, then again, I'd missed two days, and as I'd soon learn, that mattered. Like they say, everything happens for a reason.

Chapter 13

I arrived at school refreshed and relaxed on the Wednesday after my extended half-term. The weather was sunny and warm, which matched my mood perfectly as I parked the car and strolled the short distance from the car park.

There was something about the second half of the summer term that had a positive effect on both pupils and staff. Yes, it would fall apart comprehensively during the last few days of term, but at this point the promise of the long summer holidays seemed to inspire everyone to crack on and work hard. The excitement of the holidays, for the pupils at least, seemed almost physical. It meant no work, lots of play time, late nights and lie-ins. It also meant that when everyone came back in September, there would be the thrill of change, brand new uniforms, new stationery and new starts. There was therefore a real sense of carpe diem in the air. It was the half-term most beloved by almost everyone. Particularly now it had been confirmed that our OFSTED inspection had been postponed till at least the second half of the autumn term; many a teacher's summer would be all the brighter because of that, chiefly because so much less of it would need to be spent working.

'Morning!' I trilled to Barbara, the most senior of the school secretaries, as I walked by reception en route to the staff-room. She was on the phone to someone as I passed, but gestured that I should stop. I did so, musing, as I waited for her to finish, that this might be something to do with our new girl, Morgan.

'Did you have a nice break, Barbara?' I asked her, as she finally finished her call and swung her chair round to face me at her hatch. 'Is it Morgan? Have the records from her tutor come through yet?' This was something Mr Giles had assured me he'd get for me, just so we'd have some idea of what parts of the syllabuses she did and didn't know.

She shook her head. 'Oh no, Casey, there's nothing on that front yet. No, I was just asked to grab you as soon as I saw you. It's Mr Dawson, Jim. He's waiting to see you and said he'll be in the quiet room. Said it's urgent.'

The quiet room was so called because it was just off the staff-room, and away from the main hubbub as it was where the staff computers were. 'Right,' I said. 'Thanks. I was on my way to the staff-room anyway, so I'll catch him right away.'

I headed off to the staff-room, intrigued. Jim may have just wanted to brief me on what had been happening in the Unit, but my spidey senses were telling me it wasn't going to be that simple. So some sort of crisis, no doubt. Jim didn't tend to bandy words like 'urgent' around needlessly.

I wondered what urgent thing it might be. Could be something to do with Kiara of course, but it could equally be one of the others, about which I had mixed feelings; I realised I *wanted* it to be about Kiara. However much I understood the whole 'softly softly' thinking, I wanted action – I wanted the facts.

'Ah, Casey,' Jim said, springing up from one of the computer terminals as soon as I entered. 'Sit down, sit down. How was half-term? Did the move all go okay?'

I said okay, fine and yes, and batted the queries straight back at him, though I could tell there were things other than half-term small talk on his mind. 'Let me fill you in quickly,' he said, glancing at his watch, once we were both seated. 'We both need to go see Don Brabbiner before the bell goes, but as we've got the room to ourselves still, I'll catch you up first.'

'Go on, then,' I said, intrigued now, 'catch me up. What's happened?'

He pulled a face. 'I warn you, it's not pleasant. As you know,' he began, 'I was asked to replace you till today, but, as it turned out, I didn't last beyond Monday morning. Kelly had to take over – she's with Don now, by the way, giving her statement.'

'Statement? That sounds serious. Jim, what's *happened*?' My mind was already heading off over the jumps – jumping to conclusions; had Paddy Giles been down and dragged his daughter out by the hair? Jim was a male, after all.

If only. 'It was all going fine,' Jim continued. The kids were fine, no bother – that new gypsy girl, Morgan, she seemed lovely. No bother – just keen to get her head down and get on with her work. No problems at all until the lunch bell in fact. That was when the ordure hit the fan.'

'What *happened*, Jim?' I asked, willing him to hurry up and get to the point.

He looked slightly flushed; not quite himself. He ran a hand through his thatch of hair. 'What happened, Casey,' he said, 'if you want it in a nutshell, is that Kiara Bentley offered me a damn blow job!'

'*What?* I squeaked. 'Surely not. *Really?* She's only bloody 12 for God's sake! I mean I know you're telling me that she did, and I'm not doubting you for a second, but, *really*? Actually used those exact words?'

'Well, I'm certainly not bloody making it up!' Jim said, understandably tetchy.

'Sorry,' I rushed to say. 'Of *course* I don't think you're making it up. I just can't get my head round it …'

Oh God, this was all beginning to stack up, wasn't it? For me at least – was Jim even aware of Mr Bentley's allegations?

'Trust me, Casey,' he said, 'this is difficult for me to imagine too, but there you go. That's what happened.'

'I'm sorry, Jim,' I said again. 'I'm just in shock. How did it happen? Where? When?'

It seemed that Kiara had asked Jim if she could stay behind when the lunch bell went, as she needed to talk to someone about what she'd been up to during the holidays. Jim had agreed (so Gary *had* briefed him about our conversation prior to half-term) because he knew she might have stuff she needed to get off her chest. But talking, apparently, was the last thing on Kiara's mind. She'd apparently acted in a very suggestive manner, pouting and fluttering her eyelashes at him. And when he'd sat on the edge of my desk, the better to chat to her informally, she'd actually reached out and tried to stroke his leg.

At this point Jim had naturally jumped down and told her to stop being silly, then told her to run along and go and have her lunch. But Kiara was apparently having none of it. 'You can't fool me, sir,' she'd said to him. 'I know what you want, a nice blow job. I can give you one if you like. I won't tell.'

Poor Jim. This was horrible territory for a male teacher – well, for any teacher, in fact, because he was in the room alone with her. She could say anything about the encounter, and might feel inclined to do so, as he'd rebuffed her – and it would be extremely difficult for him; his word against hers. I really felt sorry for him, and didn't know what to say. Well, other than 'it'll be alright', which I knew wasn't helpful in the slightest.

No, if word got around about this to pupils and staff, it could very well put an end to his career, no matter how innocent he was. If a girl did something like this and then told all her friends, they would tell their friends, and they'd then tell their friends, and before you knew it, some parent would hear the attendant whispers and giggles and the story – the fiction – would take on another life completely, and when that happened, there'd be no coming back from it, not really, even if it was proven to be a complete fabrication.

Even if a teacher survived all that, was acquitted and managed to keep their job, the taunts never went away and the whispers in the staff-room were still present; they just got a little quieter. No, this was serious, *extremely* serious, and had to be dealt with swiftly and correctly. No wonder Jim wasn't looking quite himself.

'I honestly don't know what to say, Jim,' I said, standing up and smoothing my skirt down. 'But we'd better get along to Don's office now, I suppose. So why's Kelly in there?' I asked, having just had a thought come to me. 'Is she a witness to anything?' I added hopefully.

Jim shook his head sadly. 'If only,' he said. 'No, she's in there because she had to take the class after I reported it, and she's spoken to Kiara about it. Though I obviously don't yet know what she had to say.'

Poor, poor Jim. What a start to his week. Though it was hard to take in that Kiara would do that, there was plenty of reason to believe it. The way she'd dealt with Tommy so swiftly, and so painfully, back in that assembly. *My mum showed me how to do that.* Wasn't that what she'd said? The 'fact' of what sort of 'carer' her mum might conceivably be. That knowing, 'older than her years' look she'd always had. Tommy being so adamant that he hadn't actually said the lewd things she'd accused him of. Oh, God, oh, God, oh, God, I thought, as we hurried along to the deputy head's office. Everything about it was beginning to make my antennae start to twitch.

* * *

Two minutes later they were twitching fit to bust, just by virtue of the expression on the deputy headteacher's face. It was deemed that due to the nature of what Kiara had said subsequently there was no reason why Jim and I couldn't hear it.

At first, it seemed she'd simply denied everything. 'Vehemently, in fact,' Kelly explained. 'But come yesterday morning, it seemed that she'd had a bit of a change of heart, actually asking me if she could stay behind and talk to me at break time, and then admitting to me that she'd behaved inappropriately.'

'Thank God for that,' I couldn't help interrupting her to say.

'Indeed,' she agreed. 'But there's more. Once I pressed her about why she'd even thought of doing such a thing, she told me she knew that most men liked girls who could do blow jobs, and that Mr Dawson had been so lovely to her that she wanted to be sure he wasn't one of them.'

'Come again?' Jim said.

'A "nice" man,' Kelly supplied. 'She wanted to be sure that you were really a nice man, as opposed to the kind of men her mum knew. Testing you, in effect. She said that herself.'

I couldn't quite believe what I was hearing. 'What?' I asked. 'She actually said that, about the men her mother knew? Oh my God, so Mr Bentley *was* telling the truth then?'

'It seems so,' Donald said, and I could tell there was still more. Everyone suddenly had their Very Serious Faces on.

'Casey,' Don started, addressing me directly, 'Gary's been investigating things further, along with social services, naturally. He's just been making a couple of calls and should be with us at any moment.' He checked his watch. 'And I was thinking that perhaps it's best if Kelly goes back to look after your pupils, so that we can all sit down together and we can put you properly in the picture; Gary might well have some further updates from overnight.'

'Of course,' I said, my brain going nine to the dozen. Where was Kiara now? What 'updates' was he expecting? 'Whatever you say,' I added as Kelly left the office, thinking vaguely what a shame it was that I wasn't there for class *again*, but at the same time hungry to know what the heck was going on.

And learn I did. And the first thing I learned – and learned good – was that you should never judge a book by its cover. I felt so stupid that I'd been completely taken in by Mrs Bentley. I hated to think that I was apparently so shallow that her impressive show of ultra-cleanliness had dazzled my vision, clouding my judgement, and had prevented me from looking beyond the sterile environment she called a home.

To be fair to myself, I'd had my reservations, and I'd definitely voiced them; that feeling that I was missing something, even though I hadn't known what it was – but still, I shouldn't have left it there.

'Don't blame yourself, Casey. That's just silly,' was almost the first thing Gary said when he'd arrived and I told him how much of an idiot I felt. 'How were any of us to know? And though Jim's possibly the last person who'll thank me for saying it, it's actually a blessing that she came on to him the way she did.'

He then filled us in on what he'd since found out. In fact, what he'd already started investigating over the half-term break, by having a quiet word with a close contact of his in social services. A contact who'd revealed that Mrs Bentley had indeed been in trouble in the past for this kind of thing, but their involvement had ended several years back, after monitoring her for three years, during which time it appeared that she'd cleaned up her act and was concentrating on being a good parent to her daughter.

Gary had then done some other snooping around – he didn't go into details – and had apparently found out one of the neighbours had recently put a complaint in to the council about the stream of men going in and out of the house at all hours. The police also had a record of another neighbour (a local neighbourhood watch official) reporting a child being left alone late at night on a regular basis.

I was shocked. And not just by the facts that were being put before me. I was shocked that a jigsaw hadn't started to form in anyone's mind; that the authorities hadn't put all the pieces together. Incredible or not, though, it simply hadn't happened. The incidents were all spaced out over too long a time and no one had connected the dots. On their own, none had been serious enough to warrant removing a child, and no one had managed to put them together.

Till now. 'Now it's happening,' Gary continued, his expression grim. 'Later today, someone will be calling into school to collect Kiara, and she will be placed with a foster family till this is all sorted out.'

I gasped. For all my 'action, action, action' bluster prior to half-term, now it *was* going to be done I couldn't believe it could all happen so fast. She'd left her mum's house, come to school and then … and then what? They'd swoop in and claim her? Just physically take her away, whether she wanted to be taken away or not? It just seemed so brutal, and I couldn't quite imagine standing by while they dragged her off with them. I couldn't quite conceive that, however much she professed to hate her mum, she would just meekly trot off with strangers. I couldn't quite conceive that she did hate her mum, come to that. She was a 12-year-old girl; she'd obviously have her spats with her mother and, given the terrible state of play when it came to her parents' warring, I don't doubt she had more spats than most. But this was still her mum, and her home, and, bar her dad's place, all she knew. It seemed more than brutal, in fact. It seemed too horrible to actually be happening, and I really couldn't imagine being a part of it. What if she clung to me, traumatised, pleading for them not to take her?

But I also knew that it couldn't be any other way. I took a breath and tried to rationalise, to help calm myself down. Mrs Bentley was a prostitute and probably had been for a number of years. No matter how well she provided for her daughter financially, she was breaking the law, and, from the sounds of things – and the evidence I'd seen with my own eyes – her mother's choice of 'career' was impacting very badly on Kiara, and that was just given what we knew – there might be more.

There was more. 'Just one other thing you should know, Casey,' Gary said. He was clearly not blind to my distress at what was going to happen; to the gamut of emotions that were tumbling over one another inside my head. 'One of the neighbours I spoke to myself – and she's going to make a statement to the police, too – said that she's watched Kiara being taken out of the house very late at night, wearing her school uniform, full make-up and with her hair in pigtails. Casey,' he added, 'I think it's probably even worse than you're currently thinking. Right now, I think it's probably safe to assume that Mrs Bentley has been taking Kiara out on the streets *with* her.'

I felt sickened. And to my consternation, I felt sick as well. With my stomach empty, bar two coffees, I realised I actually felt nauseous. 'I'm sorry,' I said, standing up. 'I think I need some fresh air. I'll be okay. This is just so hard to comprehend …'

'Of course,' Don said, also standing up. 'Take as long as you need, Casey.'

I nodded and somehow made my way to the door without heaving, not quite believing that I really might throw up. I'd heard about it and read about it – but *me*? It couldn't be happening. But with the images that were insistent on invading my head, it seemed it was.

I made the staff restroom and vomited into the nearest toilet.

Chapter 14

Kiara was, at first, perfectly amenable. Two social workers arrived at the school just before the bell rang for lunch break, so that Kiara could be spoken to and taken away – how horrible that expression was – without causing too much disruption to the afternoon's class.

I had a lump sticking in my throat for the rest of the morning, naturally, and was eternally grateful that Kelly was able to hold the fort in the Unit for me, while I kept myself distracted with paperwork and lesson plans and sorting out some past papers for our new student, Morgan, who'd be my priority once lunch was over and Kiara was gone, and I could sit down and get to know her a little better.

Out with the old, in with the new – that jolly quip kept coming back to haunt me. What a strange business it had been with Kiara thus far. I'd been so adamant that something had been going on behind those enormous brown eyes; now that I'd been proved right, and between us we'd hopefully been instrumental in putting an end to something bad, I felt no sense of achievement, or indeed relief – just this hollowed-out feeling in my stomach every time the reality of what was going to happen next kicked in.

But, as I say, Kiara was at first perfectly calm about everything. Kelly brought her along to Gary's office once the lunch stampede was over, and when she saw me sitting there, she smiled. I'd been brought in so that she'd feel a little more comfortable with strangers, and though I wasn't looking forward to the trauma that was coming, I was glad to be included. I agreed it could only help.

'Hi, miss,' she said brightly, as I patted the seat of the chair next to me. 'Did your house move go okay?'

'Hi, love,' I said as she sat down, neat as a pin, as she always was. 'Yes it did. A smooth move.'

She grinned, seemingly oblivious to the two strangers present; the middle-aged woman in the purple cardigan, and the younger, bespectacled man. 'And did you get your way about the new curtains?' she asked, with a giggle.

I nodded and smiled at her, painfully aware of the lowered heads of the two social workers, and of Gary clearing his throat as an indication we should begin.

'Kiara,' he began, 'we've asked you come in to talk to us about some concerns we have. Some quite serious concerns. I'm hoping that you can listen very carefully and try to be as honest as you can when you answer me. Do you understand?'

Gary's tone was incredibly gentle, but I could see the tension appearing on Kiara's face. 'I think so, sir,' she responded, finally seeming to take in the presence of the two unsmiling strangers in the room with us. I reached across and gave her arm a squeeze of reassurance as I braced myself for what was to come.

Gary then went on to ask Kiara what she knew about what her mum did for a living and, now that she understood why we were there and seemed to get what Gary was driving at, a change came over her; almost, if it's not too fanciful, a kind of shedding of a skin. It was then that I realised that perhaps she had been waiting for just this moment – for the day to come when she could finally spill the beans, tell the truth. She must have been bursting with the keeping of such things, after all, and it suddenly struck me why she found it hard to have friends.

And out it duly came. Yes, she understood what her mum did to earn extra money. Yes, that was the reason she was sometimes out late into the night. Yes, her mum's 'friends' came to the house sometimes, but she usually stayed in her bedroom when that happened. Yes, in the last few months she went out with her mum sometimes in the evenings and yes – here she faltered, having to recount things she obviously found it traumatic to contemplate, let alone articulate – if she gave them blow jobs 'and other stuff like that – not proper sex though' – she'd be given extra pocket-money.

I was in a room with a child protection officer and two experienced social workers, who had doubtless heard such stories many, many times before. But I don't think I was the only one in that room who was physically recoiling at the images that were being painted in our minds by Kiara's words. Perhaps had she been older, more fully adolescent, physically bigger, more on the cusp of womanhood – perhaps if that were so it wouldn't feel quite so repellent. It still *would* be, of course. Any kind of sexual assault (and I counted her mother as one of the perpetrators here) is and always will be an act of violence against a woman, but sitting together in Gary's office, looking at this tiny, doll-like child, made the thought of what she'd been subjected to so much worse.

Yet Kiara herself, despite the sickening nature of what she'd disclosed to us, still had an air of lightness, of expectation, about her. And once she'd finished answering Gary's questions I realised why.

'So am I going to be allowed to go and live with my dad now?' she asked Gary. And I don't think she once thought – perhaps wouldn't have, in a million years – that the answer coming was going to be 'actually, no'.

It was, to say the least, a difficult couple of weeks for me after that, mostly because I was now completely out of the loop. Not to mention learning a valuable lesson about how child protection worked. And it did what it said on the tin. I couldn't understand this myself at first. When Gary had explained to Kiara that no, she couldn't go and live with her dad, and she'd burst out with the word 'why?' I had to clamp my mouth shut before I asked the same question. After all, she'd been staying at her dad's house regularly now, and was so obviously happy there, so I couldn't see why she couldn't just move in with him for the time being.

The opposite was to be the case, however, and the female social worker gently explained why. Social services had a duty to put Kiara in a place of safety, first and foremost, and as her father was an unknown quantity to them – however lovely Kiara said he was, she'd added, nodding her understanding that he was – until he had been thoroughly vetted and assessed by them, she couldn't be allowed to go there. Yes, in all probability she would been able to see him, and 'as soon as we can arrange it, I promise', but in the meantime it was important she was somewhere safe and secure, while they made all their enquiries. Kiara was naturally inconsolable at hearing this and, despite knowing that it was the only way to proceed in the short term, I felt I had badly let her down.

Kiara had been taken from school that same lunchtime, flanked by the two social workers, destined for the home of a 'lovely' foster family some distance away, and in floods – and I mean floods – of frightened tears. Here, at least, I could try to provide some physical comfort; it was understandable, since I'd become the person at the school to whom she'd grown most close, that she'd choose me to cling to, to entreat, to beg and beg that they didn't take her away. And how else was she expected to react? The bottom had fallen out of her world.

The social workers were gentle yet firm, understanding yet immovable; again, they had been through this process many times and I didn't doubt that it never got any easier. But, as with saying farewell to loved ones at airports, they seemed to know it was best to get it over with quickly and get away. So all I could do was try to reassure Kiara that, if she wanted, she could perhaps write to us at school; to Tommy, to Jonathan, to Chloe – specially to Chloe – and let us know how she was getting on.

'And we'll write back right away,' was the last thing I could promise her, through my own drip-drip of tears, understanding, but not quite being able to believe, that there was a good chance that her life as she knew it was over, that tonight she'd be sleeping in a stranger's bed, far away. That we might never see her again.

Two weeks on, that was the thought that was still getting to me the most. Along with the fact that I knew nothing of what was going on. Yes, Donald had promised me that he'd let me know the minute we had an update, but two weeks on there was nothing to report, other than that Mike Moore had returned and was as mortified by developments as everyone else was.

Which didn't change anything. Not that I expected to hear anything I couldn't work out by myself. My expectation, born of what I knew of how things like this usually worked, was that all I'd hear was that Kiara would be settling into a new school in a new area – that was the way fostering usually worked; get them right out of the area, away from undesirable people who might wish to contact them and vice versa – and that, depending on what position her mother took about getting her back, there would then be 'due process'; that she would perhaps have to prove to the courts that she could change her ways and become a good enough parent to have her daughter back, or (as seemed possible given Kiara's disclosures that she was herself being made to perform sex acts on 'clients') she would not.

As for Kiara's dad, I could only hope that he *would* continue to be able to see her. He might well be found wanting in terms of his living and employment situation, but my hope was that they'd see that he was keen to be a dad to her. That was key, I felt, to her emotional well-being. That and the hope that I knew would burn brightly within her, that, once the dust had settled, there was a chance that she *would* be able to live with her dad. But would she? Now social services had care and control of her, would they really feel able to put her in such a place? There was no glossing over it – it was a dump.

But now – just like that – she was no longer my problem. We'd finished what we'd started and she was gone, and that was that. It was almost the end of June now – only four weeks until we broke up for the long summer holidays, and though I was driving everyone mad at home, going on and on and on about it, I had to mentally switch gears and shift my professional focus to the kids I still had. As Mike had said at least three times in my presence (and possibly a few more times out of it), what did I expect? I was working with the challenging and challenged. This was the sort of thing that was bound to happen from time to time, and I probably needed to man up a bit.

Punching him in the chest for making such a suggestion was at least good therapy.

That and the innate ability children have for taking up all of your attention. 'Calm down, boys!' I called out as Jonathan and Tommy burst in through the doors to the playground, at the end of lunch break that Friday. It was a glorious day and I'd had my so-called 'French doors' open; it was one of the best things about my classroom. Though it did mean they moved smoothly from playground to classroom without the calming step of having to walk nicely down the corridor first. 'Play time gets left *outside* my room please, boys,' I chided. 'Time to take your seats, settle down and start to work. You two have your geography worksheets to carry on with and they need to be handed back to Mr Harris by the end of the day, so chop, chop – let's get on with it, okay?'

Next up came Morgan and Chloe. I had expected Chloe to be bereft at the sudden absence of Kiara, but it was perhaps indicative of her situation and emotional neediness that she simply transferred her undying devotion to the older girl, starting on the very afternoon Kiara had left us.

Morgan herself seemed blessed with emotional intelligence in spade loads, which was testimony to her tight-knit, loving family, no doubt, and she was proving to be giving back as much as she was getting during her all too brief (to my mind) spell in state education. She was a lovely girl, and because of the age difference between her and the other kids, all three of them seemed to see her not so much as a fellow pupil but more as a particularly 'down with the kids' classroom assistant.

Like Kiara, she seemed happy to let Chloe monopolise her, too – well, within reason. I had to monitor constantly in order to give her respite from the relentless love and cuddles, so saving her the necessity to rebuff Chloe's advances herself so she could get on with the work she was there to do to prepare her for the last of her GCSEs. She'd already done Maths and English Language, which she'd pronounced to be hard but doable, and was now revising for her favourite – English Lit.

We'd been sneaky there; though her father forbade her from being in mainstream classes, I'd been complicit in arranging for her to join a couple of special lunchtime revision classes on *Macbeth*, and would defend breaking the embargo (to the, ahem, hilt) on the grounds that they weren't 'mainstream' or, indeed, held in a classroom. The only potential snag was that only that morning I'd spotted her and a boy who'd also been attending them in *very* close conversation out in the playground.

'Can you draw me a picture, Morgie? *Please*?' Chloe was pleading as she dragged Morgan towards her desk. 'Miss, miss! Morgie's granny has a caravan, just like the gypsies do in the fairy tales, with a teeny tiny sink and a teeny tiny stove and she makes giant pots of stew on it for when they all go camping. It's just like a doll's house!' she declared excitedly, clearly enraptured by the idea of the tiny scale of it all. I got that. I felt the same as a child.

I smiled as I watched Morgan give Chloe a big hug as a crafty precursor to gently extracting herself. She was a natural around younger kids and it showed. 'Now haven't I just *told* you I'll do that for you later, you little monkey? I have studying to do, or I won't pass my last exam, will I? And then where will I be? *Later*,' she said again, smiling over in my direction. 'If Mrs Watson says it's okay, maybe we can get some paints out later, and we'll paint it together, okay?'

I mouthed a 'thank you' to Morgan as she headed to the back of the room to take her own seat, at her own desk, where her books and papers were all spread out. But Chloe wasn't done with her yet. 'And don't forget to ask your granny if I can come and play at where you're camping. I can help her with the stew. I'm good at cooking.'

I could imagine all too well the sort of picture Morgan's lifestyle painted for Chloe, the same every child has had for decades, perhaps centuries; images gleaned from folk-lore, from those very story books she mentioned: the campfires, the painted wagons, the shire horses, the open road. It was an image that was fast being replaced by another, however – though my experience of Morgan and her family had made adjustments to mine. So I was learning plenty as well.

For now, however, work was very much the order of the day and, for Chloe, this was now centred around a new-fangled gadget she'd been given; an electronic hand-held computer-style device, loaded with programmes that could be adapted to suit the age and stage of the user. They were both new-fangled and new to the school, and Kelly had taken the training course that had accompanied them, thankfully; though I knew it was an integral part of modern teaching, I loathed new technology. But even with my reticent nature regarding all things 'techno', I couldn't dispute how brilliant they were for literacy and mathematics, particularly for those with any degree of learning difficulties.

I was grateful for Kelly's input with Chloe generally. In the last couple of weeks she'd been assigned to come into the Unit every afternoon and do a session with her, and the results were proving impressive. It had meant that I could concentrate on the boys – who worked at a different level to Chloe – as well as giving Morgan the opportunity to revise unmolested. With her final exam imminent every moment in school counted.

Today, however, despite Kelly's best efforts, Chloe seemed to have ants in her pants. 'Do try to concentrate, Chloe,' Kelly scolded for the third time in what seemed like as many minutes. 'If you don't do your work with me you won't have the *time* to paint with Morgan, because the day will be done before we're finished. Now come on, sit still.'

Chloe was intent on spinning around in her chair to try and catch Morgan's attention, however, and I could see that Kelly was beginning to get cross with her. I set down my own notes and walked across to them, grateful that whatever geographical features the boys were working on were managing to hold their attention.

'What's wrong with you today, love?' I asked Chloe as I knelt down beside her. 'You're usually such a good girl when you're doing your literacy.'

She pursed her lips and pouted much like a toddler would do. Since Morgan had joined us, although her academic progress had been going well, it occurred to me that, looked at from the point of view of her maturity, emotionally she seemed to be regressing. 'I want Morgie,' she said, her lower lip sticking out, as if for emphasis. 'I want Morgie to sit with me. I don't like Miss Vickers no more.'

I glanced at poor Kelly. No teacher ever wanted to hear that, me included. 'Chloe, I know you don't mean that about Miss Vickers – you and she are good friends. Come on, what's up?' I asked her quietly. 'There's something else, isn't there?'

To my surprise, even given that this was Chloe we were talking about, she burst into tears and threw herself against me, almost knocking me over, and requiring me to grab the adjacent table to stop us both tumbling to the floor. All hope of the boys not noticing the incident was now gone. I could already hear Tommy and Jonathan sniggering from their table.

'She's a baby, miss!' Jonathan called out, quick as a flash, as was his way. 'Maybe she needs her nappy changing!' Both he and Tommy, both naturally finding this hilarious, began laughing, causing Chloe to cry more.

I shot them both a warning glance.

'I'll go over,' Kelly said, getting up from her seat, leaving me to sort out my personal limpet-mine.

'Lovey, what on earth is wrong with you today?' I asked, once I'd regained my balance and placed her gently but firmly back in her chair. I pulled out the one next to her. 'What are all these tears for?'

She could hardly speak for sobbing. 'I want Morgie,' she howled. 'I want Morgie to be my mummy, miss. She never drinks vodka, miss. She told me. Never, *ever*. So she never shouts at me, and she always gives me hugs.'

She was reaching out to me again, much like a toddler asking for a carry, so, despite her size – she was almost as big as I was – I pulled her onto my knee. It didn't escape me that I must have looked like a small ventriloquist with an extremely large dummy, but with Kelly minding the boys, I didn't expect any further quips. 'Has something happened at home, sweetie?' I asked, as she burrowed her face into my neck. 'Something different? Something new that's made you feel sad?'

Chloe shook her head and sniffed, then sighed heavily. 'I'm just so fed up, miss, that's all. I wish I had a big sister – why didn't I get a big sister? It would be alright then, wouldn't it? Because *she* could be my mummy, couldn't she? When *she* doesn't get me up, and I don't have any uniform, or there's no cereal, and my hair's a mess – I *hate* my hair miss, I *hate* it! But it wouldn't matter then, would it?'

'I know ...' I said, smoothing her hair down. 'I know ...'

But Chloe was on a roll now. 'It's not fair, miss, is it? I want to live in a caravan, like Morgie does, and have a granny who loves me like hers does.' She pulled away slightly then. 'Do you know, miss? You know when Morgie's granny makes stew? Well she even makes it for children who *aren't even her real kids*!'

Chloe had said those last words as though they were the most important of all. And perhaps they were. No, not perhaps – that was the nub of it all. That other kids weren't just loved and cherished; they were loved by grannies with so much love inside them that they even had enough left over for one and all.

It was a moment of insight that showed that, despite her learning difficulties, she was developing emotional intelligence, but it was one I didn't envy her, given her home situation. With that kind of knowledge came emotional pain – she was getting old enough to realise that having an alcoholic mother wasn't a very nice business.

I continued to hug her, wondering fleetingly about teachers and burn-out and how you kept your own emotions in check while dealing with long hours and work stress and the tyranny of the bell and – as in this case – knowing that you couldn't sort the ills of some children, however many natty hand-held devices you had at your disposal. How long before you felt unequal to the task of doing what little you could do to help?

I shook the thought from my head. That couldn't happen, not to me. This was a relatively new position, and the current job description – which seemed to change and get added to as each term passed – made it clear that I would be dealing with traumatised children over the course of my day-to-day duties. No, mine wasn't a job that could allow for sentiment to take over, let alone sentimentality.

We couldn't change her situation, just her ability to deal with it. As work mantras went, I'd heard worse.

'I know, sweetie,' I whispered into her hair, 'I know. And I promise, I will try to think of something to make things a little better for you. I promise I'll do whatever I can, okay?'

We eventually got her – and the boys as well – settled back to work then, aided and abetted by my trusty packet of biscuits. *But how?* I wondered, as I made drinks for Kelly and myself for last break. *By taking her away from her current life and giving her a new one?* With her mum's drinking that was never very far from being a possibility anyway. And now I'd seen it in action, I didn't know quite how to feel.

Well, except that I'd been blooded.

Chapter 15

Fate was watching my figure even if I wasn't. Just as I was about to dunk my first chocolate biscuit of the day, Kelly nudged me and nodded towards the classroom door. Standing outside was Gary Clark. I was surprised he didn't just walk in, as he normally did, but from what I could see of him through the glass panel, he looked quite serious, and as he gestured to me to join him out in the corridor rather than come in, I dutifully put down my biscuit and went to the door.

'Will Kelly be alright to watch them for ten minutes?' he asked when I opened it.

'Of course,' I said, mouthing a 'won't be long' back to her. I joined him outside and closed the door again and we headed back down the corridor. 'Problem?' I asked, wondering if I was being taken to the scene of some new adolescent 'crime' or fracas.

'No, no,' he said. 'Just needed to bring you up to my office for a confidential chat. Seems Kiara Bentley is coming back to us.'

'*Really?*' I said as we fell into our usual walking rhythm – Gary striding normally, with me having to incorporate the odd hop-skip-and-jump to keep up. 'Oh, that's great, Gary! But what does that mean? Have they found her a local placement? Or – oh, my God – she's not back with her mother, is she? They wouldn't let that happen, would they? Surely not? Or, don't tell me –'

Gary laughed. 'Calm down, Casey, take a flipping breath, will you? There's absolutely no point in me trying to have a confidential conversation with you, is there? Don't worry. I'll tell you everything when we get there.'

I hurried along beside him, feeling ever so slightly like a scolded child, though an unrepentant one, as I reflected that some people were born to be cool as the proverbial cucumbers and some people weren't.

'And there's no point in giving me one of those looks,' Gary added, obviously aware of my reverie. 'There could be anyone lurking in these corridors.'

'What, like spies?' I huffed. But we were there now, so he could finally spill the beans.

'She's going to her father's,' he said, once he'd followed me inside and closed the door behind us. 'It seems Mr Bentley has cleaned his act up somewhat, and social services have agreed that Kiara can move in with him for a trial period.'

'Oh, that's great news!' I said, 'When? When is she moving in with him?'

'She's already there,' Gary explained. 'Was taken to him yesterday, I'm told. She will be back in school from tomorrow – and back with you, obviously. At least till the end of term, we think, so you can monitor things.'

Gary could have told me all this at the classroom door, so I knew there must be more to come. Stuff that was too sensitive to be picked up by a stray ear. 'I sense a "but" in all this, Gary,' I said. 'Is there?'

He nodded. 'Sort of. It's just that she might be a bit delicate, Casey. According to the discussion I've just had with Jenny Davies – that's her social worker; the one you met? – during the past two weeks, Kiara has been extremely forthcoming about her life with her mother.' Gary's forehead creased then. 'It's appalling. There's no other word for it. And worse is that Jenny said she spoke almost matter-of-factly about it. This is clearly quite long established, and Kiara seems to have – what would the word be? – acclimatised? She's certainly displayed no great distress at the things she's been made to do, so there is a *lot* buried deep, I don't doubt. And the feeling is that now's the time when she might go into meltdown – now she's away from it and can start properly processing it.'

I couldn't begin to imagine how a 12-year-old would work out how to deal with something like that. 'She's so tiny, Gary,' I said. 'So *young*. I mean, where *do* you start? How do your unscramble it all from her psyche? All those things she's been subjected to ...'

'There's one positive, at least, and that's that she's apparently never been raped, so we must be grateful we were able to intervene when we did. Though she has apparently been an integral part of her mother's business – photographed in various states – presumably for marketing purposes,' he added dryly, 'and performing various other sex acts on a number of her mother's clients.'

I took a deep, slow breath. No matter how often I'd heard clues to all this over the days I'd spent with Kiara, I could never get used to the idea of what had been really going on behind that squeaky clean facade – what had been behind the hair pulling, the fatigue, that old-beyond-her-years look she always had in her eyes. Boy, how old beyond her years had she been forced to be. And who were the vile creatures for whom she performed these acts? Other girls' fathers? Much as I wished it otherwise, I knew the answer might well be yes. No wonder I could never stop the involuntary shudder as I tried to push the mental images away.

'Poor little girl,' I said. 'I don't know about feeling delicate – it's a wonder she can function at *all*. What kind of monster must that woman have been? It still doesn't quite compute. If you'd seen her place, Gary … It really just doesn't compute – there's such a disconnect in my head.'

He smiled mirthlessly. 'You've not heard of Cynthia Payne, then? Anyway, kid gloves are obviously the order of the day. She's clearly going to be a work in progress for a long time – there are all sorts of doors open to her if she wants, or needs, to talk, but no one is going to put her under any pressure. Business as usual as far as school is concerned. There's regular counselling in place via social services, but as far as we're concerned it's just carry on as per normal and keep an eye. You know the score, too many cooks and all that.'

I did. I knew what Gary was essentially saying was that it was important she wasn't overwhelmed by a surfeit of anxious, hovering adults; it was overwhelming for a child to have to revisit a painful past at the best of times, so to feel that the world and its brother were all wanting to be in the know could be difficult to handle, if not unbearable.

'At least she's now back with her dad,' I said. 'Thank goodness for small mercies. I'm really pleased for her – thank God he's come back into her life and shaped up at least. He could be key to her getting her head straight, couldn't he?'

Gary told me they all felt equally positive. That social services had spelled out the steps he'd have to take and, with their support, and a bit of necessary financial input, he'd started to take them; which might seem like questionable use of 'taxpayers' money' but, given that the alternative would be full-time foster care, was in fact the cheaper option and, in terms of Kiara's emotional health, assuming her father could sustain his current efforts, overwhelmingly the best long-term option too.

So he'd been provided with a proper bed for her bedroom and a number of other essential items, as well as being directed towards the kinds of things he needed to be aware of when caring for a child on a full-time basis. Things like providing her with a decent diet, adhering to bedtime and behaviour rules and, most of all, keeping her safe. They had also assured him that they would be on hand 24/7, for as long as he needed them to offer any other help he might require, and for as long as they felt it was necessary. He had also got himself some temporary work as a labourer on a building site, the promise being that, if he stuck at it, it might lead to a more permanent position.

All in all, though it was early days, it sounded very promising, and I couldn't be happier for Kiara, who I knew would start to heal so much better, and perhaps quicker, with her dad. I also couldn't wait to tell the others that she would be joining us again, particularly poor Chloe. Which reminded me of another issue I had to tackle.

'Gary, before I go, I just wanted to run something by you,' I said. 'Chloe Jones.'

'Ah yes,' he said. 'She's doing really well, isn't she?'

'On the surface, yes,' I agreed, 'in terms of her social skills and learning, but I'm concerned about a deterioration in her emotional state, and I was wondering if you knew someone externally who might be able to help out over the coming weeks. Once she's away from her support network here, I worry she's going to badly regress.'

'I get your point, but that's not really our job, Casey,' Gary said. 'Not once school breaks up. We can't "send the boys round" to sort her out, to put it bluntly. Or, indeed, drag her mother to AA meetings by her hair. Once we're done for the summer, it's all outside of our official jurisdiction.'

'I know,' I said, 'and I wasn't saying that we should go and stick our noses in and get into trouble – just that you might know some charitable agency or something that could help over the summer holidays. Someone with a drugs and alcohol background or even, I don't know, somewhere she could get some parenting classes maybe. Just anything we could offer really to help out. Chloe is really starting to notice now she's getting older that her mum has very poor standards when it comes to child raising, and I think she's at real risk of depression.'

Gary seemed to ponder for a few moments. 'Leave it with me, Casey. I might have one or two ideas,' he said finally. 'If I can pull something together for the school holidays, that might help some, yes?'

I grinned. I knew Gary would know someone. Some friend of a friend that could pull some strings. 'That would be more than helpful, Gary, thank you so much,' I told him.

'Payment preferred in biscuits, remember,' he said as I left.

I had been expecting Kiara to be in some way fundamentally changed when she returned; to show some clear evidence of the vile abuse she'd suffered, and to appear even more fragile and young and vulnerable than she had previously. But, of course, that was probably stupid of me. All of it had been going on, all the time, since before I'd even become aware of her, and even if not exactly under our noses, certainly enough to be responsible for that episode of self-harming the previous year.

No, it was me that had changed – me that was looking at her differently, me that was hyper-aware that she might develop some sort of post-traumatic stress disorder. PTSD was very much the term of the moment then, and as with any new 'discovery' about the human condition, professionals were bandying it about a lot and quick to use it as a label. There was nothing wrong with that – it was probably a factor in the mental malaise of tens of thousands of men returning from the trenches of the First World War, truth be told – but I still felt a little silly researching what signs I might look out for; what would suggest that, now the abuse was over, Kiara was beginning to process it – to tear down the mental wall she'd built while she was experiencing it, to protect herself, and let the distress come rushing out.

But it seemed I was barking up completely the wrong tree, because, as I observed her during the first few days of her return to the Unit, the changes I saw in her were nothing short of delightful. She rejoined us and settled back in as though she'd never been away, the only difference being the glow she had about her.

Needless to say, Chloe proved to be as fickle as the weather and, on seeing Kiara, dried her eyes and completely forgot the beloved 'gypsy' girl who'd stolen her heart and then disappeared. (Morgan, having taken her final exam, had now left us, and would only return – if allowed – for our end-of-term outing.)

I started to think that perhaps this term would end on an amazing high. Thrown together, Tommy and Jonathan had forged a friendship which had impacted positively on both of them, and Gary, bless him, had been as good as his word and been in touch with Chloe's mum. And had spoken to her quite robustly, by all accounts. Apparently he'd threatened her with an aggressive onslaught of social workers and various other teams if she didn't agree to a drugs and alcohol abuse officer going in twice a week throughout the summer holidays, to help counsel her. He'd also arranged for one of our school mentors to visit once per week especially for Chloe's benefit. She would take her on outings and picnics and give Mrs Jones the opportunity to take a breather from her various 'child care' duties, which I knew would make all the difference to both mother and child, because those six weeks could test the patience of *any* mother.

Before that, however (and to some extent we were all counting the days now), there were my final reviews to be done, on each of the children who'd spent time with us this term. This was where I would wrap up everything, summarise any achievements or any remaining weaknesses and make my recommendations about what should happen the following term. This was normally to suggest that they were ready to go back to mainstream classes or, rarely, that a child should stay with me for another half-term.

As far as my current brood went, I thought they were all pretty much ready. Chloe might well have her place confirmed at a special school before we broke up in any case, and I'd already decided that I'd recommend that Tommy be relocated to the same class as Jonathan next year. Yes, it would mean holding him back a year, but as he'd missed so much schooling, perhaps that was the right decision in any case. It would certainly benefit both boys to remain 'partners in crime', I felt, as they could support each other so well during the transition. And, as for Kiara, I could see no reason why she couldn't move back to main-stream classes too – in fact, now she was no longer in her unhappy, desperate situation, perhaps keeping her in the Unit would only be a hindrance; she was now in a position, hopefully, to begin re-forging friendships, and the sooner she did so, the better for her emotional well-being. Yes, a return to normality was very much to be desired.

In fact, I was just in the middle of recounting all that to her, when all my carefully laid plans for the summer holidays and autumn term came shuddering to a halt and slammed hard against the buffers, in the shape of a wild-eyed woman I'd never seen before.

Chapter 16

Kiara, her view half restricted by the bookcases, followed my astonished gaze, as the classroom door, which had been opened with unexpected violence, banged hard against the nearest desk.

'What on *earth* –' I began, taking in the slim forty-something woman who was paying me not the slightest amount of attention, and appeared to be on something of a mission. She looked fraught – not to mention hot; there was a damp sheeny glow about her. Unsurprisingly, as even in the June heat she was wearing a coat.

She made a beeline for the boys' table and, when she reached it, grabbed the shoulder of a startled Tommy's shirt. 'Tommy, come on,' she commanded. 'We gotta go, and we gotta go *now*. The bastard's found us. Come on – *now*! He's fucking found us!'

I emerged from where Kiara and I had been sitting, just behind the bookcases, wincing automatically at her choice of expletives in front of the children. No wonder Tommy's colourful vocabulary was so unrestrained. More importantly, I needed to regain control over the situation. 'Mrs Robinson?' I asked. Tommy's slight nod confirmed it. 'Mrs Robinson, *please*! I can see you're upset, but please don't come flying in here swearing and shouting and upsetting the children. Can we step out into the corridor, please?'

There must have been something in my tone that brought her sharply to attention. Which was gratifying. I was obviously getting the hang of this 'quiet authority' lark. She let go of Tommy's shirt. 'Look, I'm sorry,' she said, starting to try and nudge him out of his seat instead. 'Only we really do. We really *have* got to go.'

I rounded the nearest tables, walked to the door and looked out into the corridor. It being halfway through second period and, my room being where it was, you could have heard a pin drop. 'Jonathan,' I said, 'Can you shut and lock the French doors, please? And Mrs Robinson, perhaps we could have a word outside the classroom? There's nothing to worry about. There is absolutely no one around.'

'Not *here*, perhaps,' she pointed out, once she'd grudgingly come and joined me outside the classroom and introduced herself as Cathy. 'But I've left my girls round the neighbour's and we need to get moving. Honest, love, *every* second matters. I need to take Tommy out of school and I need to do it *now*.' Then, without any warning, her face seemed to fall in on itself and, with a huge gulping sigh, she burst into tears.

I put my arm around her shoulder. There was nothing of her. It was like grasping a bag of shaking sticks. The avenging Boudicca of my imaginings she wasn't, not at this moment, anyway. The door opened then, and Tommy appeared from behind it. Seeing his mum crying he threw himself at her as well. Which now made three of us, as if in a pre-match motivational huddle, Tommy and I taking it in turns to pat and say 'there, there' to the poor woman, who, now she'd started crying, couldn't seem to stop.

'Mum, shush,' he kept saying to her. 'Don't cry – we'll think of something. Where is he? How did he find us? D'you know where he is now?'

This seemed to galvanise her slightly. 'I don't bloody *know*, Tommy! That's exactly it – I don't *know*! The girls are all round Mrs Taylor's, and that's a worry in itself. What if he starts knocking on doors?' She wrung her bony hands together and I wondered if she got enough to eat. Probably not. Probably gave it to her kids. 'She's been a brick,' she said, 'but she's, like, *eighty*, and I can't have him – can't even *think* about him getting in there. Tommy, love,' she said, turning back to her son, 'I know you hate this, but what choice have we got, eh? We need to grab what we can and go. *Now*.'

'Mum, I'm sick of it!' Tommy answered, the pitch of his voice rising, as what was happening was beginning to sink in. 'Why can't you just get the cops on him like Mrs Taylor says? I *like* it here! I'm sick of running away! An' I'm not doing it no more! Get the police on him, Mum, *please*!'

'Oh, if only it was that easy!' she responded. 'Like they can just magic him away! Son, you have no idea …'

'Look, Mrs Robinson,' I said, 'I think Tommy could be right. There's a man here –'

'What would *you* know about it?' she snapped back. 'You don't know what he's like! Oh, it's all fine and dandy when they're round, promising this and that. All "Oh yes, Mrs Robinson, we'll put a restraining order on him, don't worry, and then *this*!" She scraped a hank of damp hair back from her temple, then, seeing Tommy's anguished face, quickly lowered it again. But not before I glimpsed the pearly squiggle of a scar there.

'Look,' I said again, 'at least let me take you down to Mr Clark's office. He's our Child Protection Officer –'

'I know who he is, and how is he going to help? I told you. He'll *find* us. We have to leave. Get away from here …'

'Mum, please!' Tommy pleaded. 'He might be able to do something. Please just *speak* to him, will you?'

'Please,' I echoed. 'Because Tommy could be right. That's his job, after all, and I now he knows people who can make sure you'll *all* be safe. *Honestly*. Why don't we go along for a chat – all of us, right now – and if you still feel that you have to go, then you won't have lost anything, will you?'

Tommy's mum looked as though all the fight had suddenly left her. 'Okay,' she said finally, 'but I can't see what he can do. That bastard is sneaky. He knows every loop-hole there is. And the fact that he found us proves that, doesn't it?'

'Nah, Mum,' Tommy said with what I felt showed great insight. 'It just proves that someone you trusted has a big fucking mouth! Sorry, miss,' he added.

I let it go.

I had to send Kiara haring off to track down Kelly so she could cover me, but within ten minutes I was bowing out of a rather incredulous Gary's office, leaving him and Tommy and his mum to thrash out some kind of plan; a plan I hoped and prayed didn't necessitate them doing another runner, because they could, after all, keep running for ever. At some point they had to stop. I hoped that point was now.

My only frustration – and it was a big one – was that I was once again on the periphery. Having delivered them to Gary's door I had to turn around and leave them, when every fibre of my being wanted to be in there in the thick of it, helping sort everything out. I'd seen enough of that scar to incense me and make me want to forget the language – help get that bastard what he deserved.

But if I'd thought I'd had to step away and let the professionals step in instead, to deal with the fall-out (in my job, it was ever thus), I was about to get something of a rude awakening. And if I'd thought that my day so far had been a little out of the ordinary, it was just about to get a whole lot stranger. As I hurried back to class, Kelly was waiting for me just outside the door, holding it almost closed.

'About turn,' she commanded, making a little circle with her index finger.

'What?' I asked her. 'Why?'

'You need to head back to the secretaries' office,' she explained. 'I've just had Barbara on the phone.' She lowered her voice further. 'Says you need to call Kiara's mum. She's apparently been on the phone wanting to speak to you urgently.'

'Kiara's mum? What on earth does *she* want?' I asked. 'And why the rush? I should probably find out whether I should speak to her at all – I don't know the protocol, but given the ongoing investigation ... Anyway, I can do that at lunchtime.'

'Casey, you've already lost your break twice this week, catching up with paperwork, and that's on top of losing it every Wednesday when you go over to the Reach for Success centre – I know all these things for a *fact*. Go and do it *now* – Kiara and Jonathan are absolutely fine here – probably busy gossiping, truth be known. Go and sort it now, then it's done.' She grinned at me. 'And don't hurry back. And that's an *order*!'

I did as I was told. Kelly was right. No time like the present, and as I hurried back to the admin block I wondered just what Kiara's mum *had* called about. Wondered what was happening with her, period – as far as I knew there was an ongoing investigation into her lifestyle, wasn't there? I thought back to the catalogue of pictures – part of her 'brochure'? – and wondered what sort of involvement the police currently had. At the very least, she was in big trouble for neglect and abuse, and probably a whole list of other things too. Was she calling to try and get me on side? Explain herself? What?

Gary was obviously otherwise engaged with the Robinsons, and when I fetched up at Donald's office, he wasn't there either. Off-site at an education authority meeting all day, it turned out. So that kind of put the lid on it anyway. No matter, I thought. If and when I returned Mrs Bentley's call, it would be in my own good time. I probably did need to speak to Gary first, and he had enough on his plate. So instead, I just put my head round the door of the secretaries' office to let them know I'd got the message and was on the case.

'Take this, then,' Barbara said, passing me a post-it note bearing a phone number. 'And good luck with her – what a rude, aggressive woman!'

You don't know the *half* of it, I thought as I took it from her, because obviously almost no one in school did. In fact, I was just reflecting on how much might lie beneath the surface of so many of our hundreds of families when the office phone rang again.

Jane, one of the other secretaries, answered it just as I was about to return to my classroom, when the frantic flapping of her hand stopped me. Barbara turned as well.

'Is that her again?' she said.

Jane nodded. Then she beckoned to me. 'Might as well, while you're here,' Barbara suggested. So I took the phone from Jane, more to spare her – I could hear Mrs Bentley's voice screeching at her even from a distance of a few feet away – than from any desire to communicate with her myself.

I held the receiver to my ear, intent on letting her know that I wasn't in a position to tell her anything about Kiara, but as soon as I said hello, off she went.

'Ah, you're there, are you?' she said straight away. Had she been drinking? It certainly sounded like it. 'You fucking nosey bitch!' she railed. 'You think you're so fucking clever, don't you?'

'Mrs Bentley,' I began. 'Look, I'm sorry but I can't really speak to you, I –'

''Ooh, you can't really speak to me,' she parroted back. 'Well, that's fine, because I'm not interested in anything you have to say! No, let me tell *you* something, shall I? You clever-arsed bitch. You're not half as fucking clever as you think you are.'

'Mrs Bentley –' I tried again, more firmly this time. 'I'd be grateful if –'

'Just shut up and listen for a minute, will you? She was fucking fine while she was with me and you fucking know it! No matter what I do for my fucking living. But *no*, you had to interfere.' *Fine*? I thought. *FINE?* In what warped, parallel universal might that be? 'And now she's straight out of the fucking frying pan and into the fire!'

'Mrs Bentley!' I barked at her. '*Please* try and calm down. I have no idea what you are talking about, and I won't do if you continue to scream at me like this, will I? I'm not sure you should even be calling the school.'

'I'll call who I fucking like!' she snapped. 'And you don't have any fucking idea, do you? Why? Because you're fuck-ing thick, that's why. You're fucking thick! Take her from me, and put her with him – like, I go down and he's the avenging fucking angel? Give me strength! He's a piece of fucking shit is what he is, and you are seriously going to regret this, you mark my fucking words. I hope you're hap –'

And, then, a single click. The line went dead.

I stared into the receiver like the idiot I'd just been called, and wondered what the hell that had all been about. Then at the hand that held it, which I realised was shaking.

'Well,' Barbara said. 'Gave you both barrels as well, did she? What is that woman *on*?'

'A bottle of something 40 per cent proof, would be my guess,' Jane observed, taking the phone from me and putting it back on its cradle. 'You alright, Casey?'

'I'm fine,' I lied. 'Just shell-shocked.' I dragged up a weak grin from somewhere. 'I think my ear's still ringing.'

'She's always been a funny woman, that one,' Barbara said, sniffing. 'I hope she gets everything she's got coming to her, frankly. How dare she! You sure you're alright, Casey? Nasty, having someone yell at you like that.'

Though only sticks and stones would break my bones, I thought, remembering Tommy's mum. 'It's just adrenaline,' I said. 'Natural reaction. Fight or flight and all that. I'd better get back, I suppose ...'

'Yes, but what did she say?' Barbara asked. 'What was all that *about*, exactly? Sour grapes?'

I tried to think on my feet. There would have been gossip around the school, among both pupils *and* staff –

that was all quite natural. Though no one outside the immediate circle of personnel involved would have been told more than it was necessary for them to know. Hence they'd know about the social workers, about the removal, about the return of the pupil, and, in the case of the office staff, the logistics of the case, i.e. that Kiara's 'next of kin to be contacted in an emergency' had changed a couple of times over the past few weeks. And now this. Tongues would be wagging, and that was natural as well.

'Sour grapes for sure,' I said. 'Goes with the territory. I'm the resident busy-body, poking my nose in, for – God forbid – the good of the children. Anyway, she's said her piece and hopefully that will be the end of it.'

'You wish!' Barbara said, her words accompanied by the sort of knowing grin that only a long-serving school secretary who's seen it *all* before and more can pull off with an air of complete authority.

And I knew she was probably right.

It was the end of the day before I managed to catch up with Gary again, by which time the precise meaning behind those of Mrs Bentley's words that didn't begin with 'F' had been very much occupying a corner of my mind. That and the sheer force with which a whimsical expectation about how a school term might end can be blown right out of the water.

But that was school for you. Anything could, and often did, happen, and as I'd gathered up my paperwork and filled my satchel for home, I reflected that it was perhaps all that production of adrenaline that contributed to that sense of 'burning out'. One thing was for sure – that now I worked in a school, I would never again make any kind of throwaway comment about teachers with their apparently enviably 'short days and long holidays'. In fact I felt like slinking away right there and then, and hibernating till the autumn.

Right now, however, I had to run through what Mrs Bentley had said to me, and try to figure out whether it was anything we should be worried about. After all, it had been odd – because what did she have to gain from it? From what I'd heard, she'd already made it pretty clear that if Kiara was taken away from her, then so be it – an unthinkable notion for the overwhelming majority of mothers, but, sadly, not unheard of. A tragic fact of life.

So why the call, then? What was her motivation in wanting to speak to me? Just sour grapes because she'd lost her 'assistant'?

'I think you've hit that nail on the head,' Gary said. 'I'll pass the information on to social services, of course, but I think we can assume she was just drunk and ranting.'

'She was certainly ranting,' I agreed.

'And I imagine she's under stress over the forthcoming court case. It must be galling for her, however completely deplorable what she's done, that her ex is being portrayed as the perfect father after years of not having anything to do with her. Or, I imagine, contributing a bean. But they'll review it. They're more conversant with all the facts than we are. We can let them decide what to do. And, on the plus side, it's also looking better for the Robinsons, so, in fact, it's been quite a positive day.'

He went on to explain that they were being installed in a local refuge even as we were talking, and that Mrs Robinson had been persuaded to report her ex to the police. 'We've no way of making them stay there, of course,' Gary cautioned, 'but I think Tommy himself is key there. She's obviously terrified, but now he's an adolescent – bit bigger and stronger – perhaps, I don't know, perhaps she'll feel braver. They might still do a flit, but my instinct is that his feelings on the matter might just hold sway. Let's see in the morning, eh? Keep your fingers crossed, okay? Oh, and Casey,' he added, smiling, 'go home and put *all* of it out of your mind. And that's an order.'

Obviously my day for being given orders, then. Which I was only too happy to take – as my mum would say, what would be would be ...

Chapter 17

'There should be a law against this,' I muttered to Mike as a steaming mug of coffee was nudged into place on my crowded bedside table, inches from my face and within welcome sniffing distance of my nose.

'You're such a lightweight,' he scoffed, as I opened one eye. The world seemed stupidly, annoyingly bright for 5 a.m., and I regretted the second glass of wine I'd succumbed to the previous evening. That was the trouble with decking, I decided. It inclined you to eat outside. There were so few nights in the year when you could, after all, and it *was* a minor family celebration, because Kieron had already finished his first college year and had passed his course with flying colours. But the trouble with eating outside in the evening was that it lured you into thinking you were on holiday. I opened the other eye and hauled myself upright.

'It's alright for you,' I said, to Mike's retreating back as he went off to shower. 'You're used to being up at this crazy time in the morning. My body clock feels under attack here!'

'Haha – and it's only going to get worse, love!' he quipped. I groaned. He was probably right.

Kelly was certain it was my idea. Absolutely certain. I maintained it had been Jim's, and Jim maintained it had been Kelly's, so, between us no-one was prepared to admit responsibility for our end-of-term outing taking place at a centre that was a good 20 miles away and where there was a very real risk of one of us pulling something we shouldn't.

Well, Jim and I, at any rate – Kelly, being so young and lithe, would be just fine. So perhaps it was Kelly's idea after all. It was three days before the end of the summer term now, and we were off to one of those huge outward bound centres, buried deep in some dark forest, with all sorts of outdoorsy, Duke-of-Edinburgh-awardy, scary-looking activities – all designed for maximum thrills, if not spills. No spills; they were clear on that at least, because safety was 'paramount and completely guaranteed'.

Hmm. I felt only partly comforted by that, because most of what was on offer looked terrifying. There was a big outdoor climbing wall, a traditional-style army assault course, as well as high ropes and standing platforms and stepping 'stone' courses, way up in the air, and all sorts of other lofty, tree-based challenges, all of which were minutely detailed in the glossy brochures, showing lots of colour photographs of delighted-looking children, wearing hard hats and harnesses and beaming down from on high.

And at no point was it ever suggested that the three of us had to join in, but I knew – I just knew – we'd be coerced into doing something, because that was just the way these things happened.

But that was a while away yet – first I had to negotiate my mug of coffee, pack a lunch, grab a shower, then pick up Kiara before heading to school to meet the minibus.

There were eight of us going – my four Unit children, plus Jim, Kelly and I, as well as Morgan, who had been given a special dispensation to return to school for it; something that had involved Granny Giles threatening her father with a very big stick if he didn't let her. Granny Giles was definitely my kind of woman. And, despite my baulking slightly at the early start, and the lengthier than sensible journey, the kids' excitement about it was reason enough to suffer such vicissitudes, pop a travel sickness pill and get on with it. It would be fun when we got to it. As long as I came home in one piece.

I chose some suitable clothing while waiting for Mike to come out of the shower, and, as had been happening here and there lately, my mind returned to Kiara's situation and *that* phone call. We'd not heard another peep from Mrs Bentley, and as far as I knew there had been no further development, but I was glad I'd offered to come and pick Kiara up to go on the trip (it was too early for the school bus, obviously) because I might get a chance, particularly as I'd been generous with my timings, to have a quiet chat with her on our own; one which might shed more light on what her mother had said about her dad. It was her choice of words that kept nudging at me – *out of the frying pan and into the fire.* There was something about what she'd said that had taken me right back to when I'd first met Kiara – that same itch I'd tried to scratch, and kept itching nonetheless. Deep down, I didn't quite agree with Gary's take on things; that was the bottom line. There was something else, I was sure of it – something social services might not know.

'Well, let's look at the evidence you've already given me,' Mike had said, when I'd talked to him about it. 'He's still mostly unemployed, though he's perfectly articulate and reasonably personable, and doesn't have any apparent learning difficulties. He's living in a rented flat in relative squalor, he's middle aged but seems to have the life skills of a teenager, lives off junk food and seems to have the motivation of a particularly demotivated slug. I wonder if he's a dopehead? Just an educated guess …'

And, of course, it was a pretty sensible guess. Kiara's dad was nothing like the vulnerable adults I'd spent years working with for the council. He just seemed like one of life's drop-outs. And everybody knew that an addiction to substances like cannabis could, though not in the same league as the sure-fire killer drugs like heroin and crack cocaine, still cause a person to lose all ambition and become almost completely non-productive.

And, yes, he'd been vetted and interviewed, and had cleaned up his home a bit, and there was no doubt that Kiara had blossomed now she was back with him, but monitoring the situation was only that – monitoring. Plenty of scope for someone who put their mind to it to maintain an unsavoury habit in between. After all, what did Mr Bentley do when Kiara was at school and he wasn't at work? Stalk the job centre, looking for a better job than he'd currently managed to find as a labourer on an 'as and when' basis, or see his dealer and get routinely stoned?

It was all of it – every bit of it – just idle conjecture, and perhaps I should stop imagining negative scenarios in my head. Kiara seemed to be thriving, and Mrs Bentley's rant was just probably revenge – tit-for-tat stuff, as Gary had said. Though what had prompted it – bar her being drunk, perhaps – was a mystery in itself, and I kept coming back to the same question – since she was perfectly happy to relinquish her daughter, why this sudden need to dish the dirt all this time later? It didn't really seem to make sense.

Perhaps she was just keen to get back at her apparently feckless former partner and, fuelled by alcohol, made the call to me on impulse. I pondered it all as I pulled out my heavy-duty boots and placed them atop my jeans and T-shirt. Perhaps she just grabbed a chance to boot him in the proverbials. Wasn't that supposed to be her speciality anyway?

There wasn't so much as a wisp of cloud in the sky as I pulled up in a space across the road from Kiara's dad's house, and in the bright light of a perfect summer morning, just after dawn, perhaps anywhere would show its best face. The house itself, bathed in sunshine that winked off the windows, looked a little different to how it had when I'd last come to visit, with the bins in a neat row behind the low, crumbling wall, and the buddleia and other weeds now all gone. I had no idea if this was anything to do with Mr Bentley and/or social services, but it was cheering to see that at least one 'act' had been cleaned up – a process that had presumably being going on indoors as well.

Kiara must have been looking out for me because there was no need for me to get out of the car and go and ring the buzzer. The front door opened and she emerged almost as soon as I'd switched the engine off. There was no sign of her dad, however, so I immediately switched it on again.

It was only the second time I'd seen Kiara out of her school uniform, and her outfit of skinny jeans – with artfully ripped knees – pale pink T-shirt and matching pink trainers made her look much more like the teen she was soon going to be – just after school broke up for summer if I remembered rightly. She waved back at the upstairs front window as she crossed the road, and though I couldn't see him, due to the sun winking off the window panes, I assumed Dad was there and waving back.

I was disappointed because I'd have liked to have seen him for myself, but it was early, I supposed, and there was no reason for him to come down – well, bar common courtesy, in order to thank me for picking his daughter up. *Stop it*, I told myself, mentally readjusting my position. A few social faux pas do not necessarily a ne'er-do-well make.

Kiara jumped in. 'You look nice, love,' I said.

She beamed. I think she knew it, too, bless her. 'Thank you!' she trilled. 'These are my new jeans Dad bought me.

And I remembered my lunch, miss,' she added, grinning as she waggled her bag. It was another backpack, but a smaller one; the kind kids use when going swimming. 'Peanut-butter sandwiches, for extra energy,' she explained. 'Oh and Dad said to thank you soooo much. He's really grateful. He's got a shift at the building site in a bit, so this is a real help. He'd have come down, but he's not showered yet and his dressing gown is, like, *such* an embarrassment, so I wouldn't let him.'

She giggled. So that was me told.

The journey to school wasn't a long one and as we set off I wondered quite how to start a conversation that, if I wasn't careful, might immediately alert Kiara to the idea that I was fishing for facts. But I didn't wonder long. Kiara placed the answer right in my lap.

'Is Mr Dawson coming today?' she asked me once we'd dispatched the usual dialogue about how lovely the weather was, what I had in my own lunch box – rather boringly, just an egg sandwich and a bag of crisps – and how exciting, if slightly scary, the day was going to be.

'Yes, love,' I said. 'He is. But don't be anxious about that. All water under the bridge now. It's fine.'

'I just feel so embarrassed about it all,' she said, reaching into the bag between her knees. She pulled out a little cloth purse and opened it.

'I know,' I said. 'But he's a teacher, remember. A professional. He knows the circumstances. And perhaps this will be a chance to build bridges – which is appropriate, isn't it? Given we'll be crossing some rope ones, God help us – and you can stick close to me anyway, if that'll help.'

'It'll help sooo much,' she said. 'Thanks, miss. I just cringe every time I think about it.'

I watched her pull out what was probably a chapstick but actually looked more like a pale pink lipstick, then flip down the sun visor to apply it. It made my mind immediately return to her 'outings' with her mother, particularly as I noticed the precise way she used it; with a chapstick, you normally just sling it on, unseen, but she used deft strokes to define the two bows of her top lip, like a woman would if applying a vivid scarlet. It was a sharp poke in the ribs for me. A reminder that someone had stolen her childhood.

'I'm sure you do, Kiara,' I told her, 'but you know, you must try and put it behind you, as I'm sure your counsellors have told you. Those days are gone now ...'

'I wouldn't have actually done it, you know, miss,' she said, putting the chapstick back in her bag and flipping the visor back up. 'I never would have done it.'

'I know,' I said. 'I didn't think that for a minute.' Which wasn't quite true. I didn't know any such thing. I didn't know the detail of her various forays to get clients with her mother and on balance I was glad *not* to.

'I was only testing him, that was all,' she continued, as we approached the school gates. There was no sign of any of the others or the minibus yet. Good.

'Testing him?' I asked her. 'In what way?'

'Just to know,' she said. 'Just to check if he was a safe man or a bad man. You never know. You can never tell from looking.'

I felt another mental poke in the ribs. 'Clients'. They came in all shapes and sizes, all creeds and colours. It had often struck me how impossible it was to tell who bought sex from prostitutes. Not from looking. I got that. You really could never tell.

'So that was how you went about it?' I asked her.

Kiara nodded as I pulled up in the staff car park, in the corner nearest to the school itself. 'Like I said to the social worker lady, I would never have actually done it, not even if he'd said yes. I just wanted to know that he'd say no, that was all.'

I undid my seat belt and swivelled in my seat. 'Ah, I see. I get it,' I said. 'But, love, what do you mean by "a safe man or a bad man"?'

She looked as if she was surprised that she even had to explain it. And, of course, she didn't. But I wanted to hear it described in her own words. She obliged. 'The bad men are the ones like Mum brought home. They want you to do stuff to them –' she nodded towards her lap, pulling a face – 'and it's disgusting. My dad's told me all about them now. *And* how to spot them.'

'Your dad?' I pricked my ears up. Perhaps he was being more proactive in protecting his young daughter than I thought. A helpful brownie point that would help me to re-position him more favourably in my brain. 'And what does he say about it?'

'That safe men – like him, and like Mr Dawson,' she added, 'they would never, *ever* make you do things like that for money. It's just the bad men that do things like that. That's why if you ask them you can tell. You can tell in their faces when you say it. Like, *so* easily. Anyway, I don't have to worry any more, miss,' she said, pulling together the drawstring on her bag, ready. 'Because dad's my *only* man now, for ever.'

'For ever?' I asked, smiling at her. 'I'm not sure about that. One day soon, in a year or two, you'll see a boy across a crowded room …'

'No chance,' she said immediately. 'He *is*, miss. For ever. He'd never hurt me. He's gentle. He really loves me. He loves me *much* more than he ever loved my mum.'

The poke in the ribs had suddenly become a hefty punch in my gut. *He'd never hurt me. He's gentle. He's GENTLE.* The word – that word particularly – dislodged itself from the others, and settled in the pit of my stomach, with a whump. This couldn't be happening. What I was suddenly thinking. It couldn't be right, what I was thinking, could it? *Could* it?

'Gentle?' I asked.

'*Always*,' she confirmed. I could hardly bear to look at her in case of what I might see in her face. That, oh, so-knowing face. I didn't. I stared ahead again.

'Kiara,' I said next, and as lightly as I could – so lightly that my words could almost have been carried out of the car window and away on the breeze. As if I'd never said them. Never had to. And how I wished they would. 'Do you do some of those things with your dad?'

Now I did turn. She looked shocked. 'No, of course not!' she said, almost indignantly. 'Don't be silly, miss. I told you, my dad *loves* me. When *we* do it, it's called making love.'

Chapter 18

In years to come, sad to say, I would hear things, and witness things, and deal with the fall-out from things that no child should ever have to endure. In years to come hearing things of the kind Kiara had just said to me would still affect me deeply, but with greater experience under my belt and greater exposure to life's horrors, I would have registered the enormity of it without gasping or cringing or flinching. I would have merely listened, filed it away in a temporary storage facility in my brain and then, at the earliest opportunity (I never waited), I would open up an official log book and record everything I'd been told, in as much detail as I could remember and, where at all possible, verbatim. I would do this calmly, in a measured way, conscious of the importance of following protocol in the case of a looked-after child making a 'disclosure'.

But that was for the future. Right now, it was difficult not to gape at Kiara, mouth *Oh, my God!*, and feel fearful that I'd be violently sick again.

It was okay. I knew I wouldn't actually *be* sick, because that level of shock had already happened to me. Which was in itself interesting; had I already become slightly desensitised to the sheer gut-churning vileness of the deeds that were being done to her? In any event, I was still nauseous enough to have to take a couple of deep breaths, grateful for the fact that as soon as she'd delivered her bombshell, Kiara had undone her own seatbelt, opened the passenger door and started getting out of the car. And why would she not do that? We were having a little 'girl-to-girl' chat and her comment had been throwaway, I felt sure of it. All she'd done was to gently put this misinformed older woman straight on the relationship between love and sex where her loving, *gentle* dad was concerned.

I gripped the wheel, appalled and stunned, my brain once again flooded by images that I really didn't want parking themselves up there.

'Hiyah!' I heard her calling over the roof of the car. Someone else had obviously arrived now. Best get on, then. Acting on autopilot, I reached into the back for my own backpack, groaning automatically as I hefted it one-handed into the front of the car with me, rueing (in the midst of the grisly peep show in my head) my insistence on packing everything bar the kitchen sink, just in case.

There was one thing missing, of course, and that was a big stick like Granny Giles had, which was perhaps just as well. Because I think I really could have jumped back into the car, driven round to Kiara's new and lovely, loving home, and beaten Mr Bentley to a pulp with it – my response to his evil was that visceral.

I climbed out too. Kiara had been calling out to Chloe, who'd been dropped off by a taxi, presumably as it was so early, and who was now running across the staff car park hell for leather, the better to suffocate Kiara with a hug.

I tried to think on my feet, since I was now upright, with the blood rushing between my ears. What to do next? What to do now? Now this minute?

Nothing, came the answer from my brain. Do absolutely nothing. Stick with the programme and the plan, enjoy the day out at the adventure place, do nothing to cause alarm or distress to Kiara, don't potentially precipitate any sort of scene – rock the rock wall, in other words, but do *not* rock the boat.

I took a final deep breath and went across to meet the others.

It only took a few minutes for me to realise that my Plan A had one enormous flaw. If we went off in the minibus as planned and I did nothing till I was back in school and could sit down with Gary and Mike, that would mean taking Kiara straight back to where I'd collected her from this morning.

I thought of her looking so trim and pretty in her skinnies and pink T-shirt. And felt newly nauseous. Nope. There was no way I was going to do that in a million years. *God*, I thought, as I made my way across to the newly arrived minivan, driven round from the back by Kelly: she knew. Kiara's mum *knew* – or at least had a bloody good idea. No, I thought, as I waved gaily at Kelly, she knew. She *had* to know. So why hadn't she gone as far as actually saying so to me?

Then I remembered the click that had cut her off mid-rant. Perhaps she'd been even drunker than she'd seemed. Perhaps she hadn't meant to stop when she had. And just perhaps, hard though it was to think about, she didn't call back because, in the end, she didn't care *that* much. After all, who knew how long it would have been till she progressed Kiara on to those of her clients who were after a greater range of 'services'? Not very long was my view. And it was in that moment that it struck me that Gary had probably been right. She had called to even the balance sheet, and in reality it probably was born out of sour grapes – he'd turned up again, and had the audacity to snatch away a part of her livelihood – had the audacity to come along and snatch their daughter for himself.

And nobody, not a single one of us, had had so much as an inkling of what might be – clearly *was* – going on behind that scuffed wooden front door. To think I'd been worrying about him having a few cannabis plants growing under lamps somewhere. How lightweight a crime that suddenly seemed by comparison! I thought of the ratty mattress I'd glimpsed in what I'd naïvely thought of as Kiara's room – of course it was a ratty mattress. It didn't need to be a proper bed because no one slept on it. Well, hadn't done for a while, I thought grimly; not once her father had coaxed her, oh so gently, into his bed.

Get your head straight, I told myself sternly. Letting my imagination run away with me served no purpose bar putting my stomach on a spin-cycle. I needed to decide what to do. But my Plan B – to speak to Mike or Gary *now* – was equally unworkable. It was only 6.45, which meant neither would be here for at least an hour. And there was no question of waiting till then because our timings had been precisely worked out. If we didn't get away now, we'd spend half the morning getting there, embroiled, as we knew we would be, in rush-hour traffic.

Which left a Plan C of biting the bullet and keeping Kiara back in school with me – which would mean she'd miss the trip – or a Plan D: continue as planned and get hold of either man by phone as soon as we got there. There were bound to be mobile-phone signal problems but I knew they would have a land line in their office, because I'd called it to book the thing myself.

Plan D, then. There was nothing for it. A and B were unworkable and C was as well, too cruel a blow for the poor child. I'd say nothing to anyone and once we were there I would make the call.

'I am so gonna be first up that climbing wall,' Tommy declared, as, all present and correct and with Jim now at the wheel, we headed off to the motorway and, as Kelly had coined it, to our date with derring-do.

'You're so not,' Chloe told him. 'Jonathan is.' (Jonathan having found favour with Chloe the previous afternoon by letting her brush his hair after she'd finished her own.)

'It's going to be neither of you,' Kiara corrected them. '*I'm* best at climbing. My dad works on a building site and he's taken me up his ladders so we could sit at the top of a *whole* block of flats and see the stars.'

'He never,' Tommy retorted. 'He wouldn't be allowed. And they'd 'ave it locked up and guard dogs patrolling and everything so he'd never get in anyway.'

'Well, for your information, we *did*,' Kiara shot back. 'He knows the secret entrance, and he doesn't worry about silly things like rules anyway.'

Quite, I thought wretchedly.

Luckily, once we got there, and the admin had all been dealt with, it looked like the centre staff who'd been allocated to us would take charge of the first part, which was to do the high-level treetop assault course that we'd glimpsed from the minibus on our final approach and had generally been declared to be well wicked-looking.

And you obviously didn't need to be a child to appreciate it. The two young bearded guys responsible for getting everyone kitted out and doing the safety briefing and so on looked like they'd happily do the jobs they did without pay, they were that enthusiastic.

I wished I could share their uncomplicated good humour, and on another day I would have, but it had been hard enough trying to act all jolly and 'sing-alongy' on the mini-bus. But I was soon to be able to escape – and I was beginning to feel like some sort of chief executioner – because they immediately sent Jim and me off to get cups of coffee, though not Kelly, the taller of them quipping that they'd assumed Kelly was one of the pupils, causing much hilarity all round and some heavily batted lashes; she was on the right side of the divide between wishing you looked older and being profoundly grateful if anyone snipped a couple of years off your age.

'Do the high ropes with them anyway, Kelly,' I told her. 'You'll make a nice even six, then.'

She looked thrilled at the prospect. 'Are you sure, Mrs Watson?'

'Yessss!!!' all the children shouted! Kelly shook her head, looking about as sincere about not wanting to do it as a snake-oil salesman would. 'No, no,' she said. 'No, no. I'm here to watch *all* of you doing it. It's fine.'

I pulled rank on her then. Because why shouldn't she get up there and do it with them? I couldn't think of a single reason. And it would make the children's day for them. On balance, a major plus point. 'No,' I said. 'You're doing it. And that's an order.'

And within ten minutes or so, while Jim and I took charge of their various encumbrances – lunchboxes, jumpers, just-in-case cagoules and so on – they'd all trooped off to get harnessed up, returning in the obligatory safety helmets, and accompanied by much clinking and clanking of carabiners, and with the odd look of naked fear crossing the odd unlikely face.

'Can't you come up, too, miss?' Kiara asked me, as they all reassembled.

I shook my head. 'Not for this bit. I don't do heights,' I told her. 'As you can see,' I added, patting the top of my head. 'I'm not born for them. I get dizzy. This afternoon, though. Perhaps. They've got a toddlers' assault course somewhere here, haven't they? Much more my kind of thing.'

Kiara grinned at me. 'You're not *scared*, are you, miss?' she joked.

How I hated knowing how soon she would have the smile wiped off that pretty face.

'I thought you seemed preoccupied,' said Jim as we hurried across to the office building and café with the kids' bags, after I'd briefly filled him in as we saw them off into the woods. He found a choice word to describe Mr Bentley and used it. Then used it again, as, like me, the icky reality of it began properly sinking in; I didn't doubt his own experience with Kiara brought it home to him even more.

There was no point him hanging around with me while I got hold of Gary, so once we'd stashed the bags in a room they'd allocated for school parties, he headed off to catch the children up while I made the call. Once I was done I'd go and join him, not least in my role of official photographer of my little gang. And, once again, I had the grim thought that today's antics would be a watershed for one of them, marking the point at which Kiara's life took her on a completely new trajectory. And where the last time had turned out to be something of a trial run, this time, I knew, would be permanent; no going back. It was the end of life as she had known it, and everyone in it would cease to be a part of it from today.

'You're getting a little ahead of yourself, aren't you?' Gary observed when Barbara the secretary put me through to his extension and I blurted out the gist of what Kiara had disclosed. 'Social services won't just swoop in and remove her based on what you've told me. Kids say all sorts of things, remember – but we can't automatically just assume that they're true.'

'WHAT?' I squeaked. 'She just sat there and calmly told me they made love!'

'Which is something she could be fantasising about …' Gary was quick to point out. 'A girl of her age, with every-thing she's been through – like I say, it's a complicated business.'

'It's true, Gary. I *know* it's true. I've never felt so sure of anything.'

'And you might well be right – for what it's worth, you probably are right, at least to an extent. But what's to say the boot isn't on the other foot – that she's been coming on to him? She's been sexualised, remember; involved in prostitution at a very young age. The boundaries are all blurred for her around what's appropriate and what isn't. And don't forget that he's returned to her life only recently; lots of girls have crushes on their dad when they hit puberty – it's a perfectly natural phenomenon. But if you add in the newness of their relationship, and the heightened emotions she must be feeling, *then* add in the fact that she's been so desperate to live with him – let's just say it might not be quite as black and white as you might think.'

I hadn't thought of any of that. *Why* hadn't I? I had so much to learn still. Everything Gary said had an uncomfortable credibility about it. And what did I have? My trusty spidey sense. And that was pretty much all.

But I trusted it. Trusted it totally. Yes, I'd been wrong up to now, in accepting the surface impressions. But on this, knowing Kiara better now, and having met all interested parties, I trusted my instinct completely. 'But even if Kiara *has* been the instigator of a sexual relationship between them – and I do get that it's possible, however unpalatable – it doesn't make any difference, surely? If he had concerns she was coming onto him sexually, he should share them with the social worker, shouldn't he?'

'In theory, yes,' Gary said. 'But he might be reticent about doing that. I think *I* would be in his shoes – don't forget, it would be his word against hers.'

Another perfectly valid point. 'So what about her mum? Perhaps you could speak to her, ask her to explain what she meant when she said those things to me. What she meant when she said "out of the frying pan, into the fire". It's got to be worth speaking to her, hasn't it?'

'Well, I think the first thing I'm going to do is put all this in front of the social worker. That's obviously the way to move on this – and perhaps they will speak to Kiara's mum and see what they can glean. In the meantime, go and enjoy your day ...'

'As if! With this hanging over me!'

'Go and *try* to enjoy your day. I'll get back to you as soon as I can. You have your mobile, I'm assuming?'

'Yes. Signal's patchy though. I'm calling from the office here.'

'Okay. I'll try your mobile. And if no luck, I'll send you a text. In any event, if you've not heard back by, say, early p.m., call me again. Don't worry, Casey. I'm on it.'

'Well, I hope social services are too. Because I'm the one that's supposed to be dropping her back to him at the end of the day. And you know I'm not sure I'm going to be able to do it.'

'I'm on it,' Gary said again. So I had to be satisfied with that. I hurried off, pulling the official school camera out of my backpack as I ran, so I could 'capture the moment'. In a collection of pictures I'd find it difficult to look at again.

Chapter 19

It was a text that came from Gary in the end, at around two in the afternoon. We'd not long finished lunch and the kids were off to do the climbing wall and, for those with any remaining energy, the army assault course. I'd said nothing to Kelly by this time, because there wasn't yet any point, and there was definitely no point in both of us being afflicted by that heavy, leaden feeling you always tended to get when you knew you had to be involved in something that was going to be unpleasant but that there was no prospect of wriggling out of.

'Oh, you've got a signal, then,' she observed as the phone tootled from inside my backpack.

'Seems so,' I said, wondering what it might say. I pulled it out, at which point Chloe asked Kelly if she'd go with her to the toilets, and I gave thanks that, assuming it *was* Gary who'd sent the text, I'd be able to keep it to myself for at least the rest of the outing.

It was. *U were right*, the text said. *Call me if U can. If not, we'll CU@school*. This was back in the days when a whole shortened vocabulary had sprung up for texting, now long extinct. Something invented by teenagers and, looking down at it, making us middle-aged texters sound adolescent too – as if our parents, on seeing what we'd written, would chastise us: 'Whatever happened to proper spelling? Tsk!'

I texted back 'OK', then looked over at Jim glumly, and made the decision to slip away and call Gary as soon as they'd headed off to the assault course. In just over an hour we'd be on our way back, and I wasn't quite sure how to handle things. Should I forewarn her? Give her a chance to prepare herself on the way home? I tried to imagine the scene on the minibus if I did that, and I couldn't. Every instinct, in fact, told me to do nothing – to just let it happen. But at the same time, doing nothing just felt so wrong.

Why today of all days, as well? Could there really be a worse day for this to happen? But then I reminded myself why I'd been so keen to pick Kiara up this morning. It was precisely so I'd be in a position to have a chat with her, if a chat was what she felt like having – trouble was, what I'd *really* been hopeful of doing, was putting my niggling concerns, the result of my spidey sense, to bed. I'd actively been seeking answers to a question I'd posed myself – but, *God*, had I been asking myself the wrong question!

And now I had my answer. QED.

It was every bit as bad as I'd expected it to be – worse, in fact. I'd been braced all the way home, even as I joined in with the singing, but when we pulled into the school entrance I was mortified to see that Gary was *actually standing out front* with Kiara's social worker, together with a man – presumably someone else from social services – who I hadn't seen before.

So it would probably be played out in the car park, I thought miserably, because as the minibus turned, and Kiara saw the reception committee, she placed both hands on the window and gaped. I was sitting behind her, next to Morgan – she was sitting with Chloe – and I could almost sense the vibration as her mind began to whirr. Then she turned to me. 'Miss, what's going on? What's happened? What are they doing here?'

I had no idea what to say to her, which made me feel more unequal to my job than I'd ever been before. 'Kiara, I ...' I began. *Kiara, I don't know?* Could I force that lie out of my mouth? 'Oh, love ...' I tried again, as she spun around again.

'Miss, what's going on?' she said again, the pitch of her voice rising. The minibus shuddered to a halt. 'Miss,' she shrieked. '*Tell* me!'

The other children, all bemused now, and with their own thoughts probably whirring, stood up, gathered bags and coats, and, following Kelly's brisk directive, started shuffling forwards, to the front of the minibus. Kelly looked over the seats at me, and all I could do was sigh regretfully, and I now wished I *had* filled her in.

As it was, all I could hope was that there would be no ugly scene. That we'd be able to take Kiara inside, explain what was happening to her in private and, though I didn't think in a million years that she'd go with them willingly, that it could be done without her getting into too much of a state.

Which was naïve of me. 'Come on, love,' I said, as she remained transfixed by the minibus window. There were just the two of us left on board now, Jim having known what needed to be done here, and having, along with Kelly, ushered the others away.

'They're going to take me away again, aren't they?' she said, her voice now a whisper, quashing my faint hope that she wouldn't immediately leap to that conclusion. Of course she would leap to that conclusion; that was exactly what had happened last time a brace of social workers turned up at school, wasn't it? So there was no point in trying to sugar the pill. 'To take you back into care,' I said quietly, 'yes.'

She turned to face me. 'But *why*, miss? I don't understand. *Why?* My dad's taking care of me, isn't he? Is it my cow of a mother?' She seemed galvanised by this thought. 'It's *her*, telling on him, isn't it?'

'Kiara, come on. We need to go and talk to them, sweetheart. They'll explain everything to you.' I moved to take her hand, but she batted me away.

'Explain *what?* He's *been* taking care of me. We're fine. I want to stay there! I'm not going. I'm *not going! They can't make me!*'

I became aware of the minibus rocking slightly and turned to see Gary climbing aboard. 'Kiara, love,' I said again, groping for some words that might help. But there were none that would make any of this any better. 'Kiara, I know you love your dad, and that you think he loves you, and I know this is all *incredibly* painful for you to hear, but, love, the things you do together … the things in bed … well …' I was finding it difficult to get the words out, because my mouth and throat felt so parched. 'Well, they are *bad* things, Kiara. Things he shouldn't be doing with you. He is your *father*, Kiara, and he shouldn't …'

'You!' she cried, her eyes wide with realisation. 'You! It was *you*!'

Gary began moving up the minibus, his expression grim. 'Kiara,' he said, 'I'm so sorry, but –'

'I'm not going!' she shrieked at him, grabbing her bag and shuffling out of her seat. I was sitting sideways in the seat on the other side of the aisle and, confident Gary would arrest her progress, let him block her way. Which he might have done, had she not screamed 'Don't you dare touch me!' as he tried to place a gentle hand on her shoulder – and as it was she was out of the minibus in seconds.

'Shit!' he said under his breath, turning to chase her, with me close behind him, as she jumped down the steps and started sprinting off towards the open school gates.

'*Shit*,' he said again, clambering down. 'Mike! Try and head her off!' but I could see there was little chance of either of them catching up with her. She was fleet as a fox and a good few yards ahead. And beyond the gates the main road loomed. I set off after her as well.

Fate was with us, however, because, in her haste to escape, Kiara took a short cut through our patch of 'garden', in reality a single elderly oak and some long-dead grass, which was once a year accessorised by half a dozen daffodils. It saved us. She tripped on a tree root and went headlong into a vacant parking space adjacent, giving us all the precious seconds we needed to catch her.

And that would be my memory of her, as I tried to hold and soothe her and she fought and fought against me ... the fresh rip in the right knee of her new skinny jeans and the smear of filth and oil across her baby pink T-shirt.

And then there she was, gone. There was almost everyone gone, in fact. Well, bar myself, the headmaster and Gary Clark.

I slipped to the staff toilets to freshen up, as did Mike Moore, and I also took the opportunity to call home. I only got myself at the other end of the line, chirpily telling me no one was home and that I was the burglar, but at least it reminded me that there *was* a jolly home to return to after the inevitable post-mortem, which, once Gary had finished making calls to various people, I had already been summoned to.

'Will she be coming back?' was the first thing I wanted to know once Gary, Mike and I had assembled in Mike's office. 'To this school, I mean? Ever? Is that it for good now?'

It was even more shocking than it had been the last time, because this time it really was so final. When she'd been taken from her mother's to go and stay with the foster family, she'd at least the knowledge that, all being well, she'd be allowed regular contact with her dad. But not this time. She was all out of parents now, it seemed. This really *was* it. For keeps. Whole new life.

And Kiara knew it. The devastating look she'd had on her face as she was led away to begin it had made a bore-hole into my soul. It was really upsetting me. Stupidly so – just thinking about her jumping into my car, a vision in pink, wreathed in smiles, waving up to her father, skipping away, looking forward to coming home and telling him all about it – oh, I could so easily bring all those images to mind. And now gone – no going home, no watching telly together on the re-covered sofa. Because he'd gone and killed it – killed all the good things she thought she now had in her life, with his filthy, perverted notions of 'love'.

Which was why it had to be done; why there could be no unravelling, no supervised contact, no point in the process that had already begun happening that would allow so much as a chink of him to remain in her young life. 'But he loves me! You can't do this!' She'd kept saying it over and over. But, of course, nobody could begin to explain in words she could understand, even if she heard them, that the nature of love – fatherly love – wasn't *like* that.

And Kiara hated me for it. I knew that. For being the one to whom she'd accidentally opened the trapdoor, only to reveal the hell-hole, and however much I knew I'd been acting in her very best interests, the opportunity to tell her so, to try and explain to her, was now lost to me. Oh, I could write to her, I knew that, but I so wanted to be able to sit her down and tell her face to face.

Mike Moore shook his head. 'I'm afraid not, Casey, not this time. I would be lovely if she could stay here, at least till she's on a more even keel, and perhaps if the summer holidays weren't imminent, they'd sort something temporary out – at least till the end of term. But not long term, no. The family that had Kiara last time are more than happy to have her again, long term, and as she knows them it wouldn't make sense to try and shift her elsewhere right now. She has enough to adjust to as it is, doesn't she? No, one good thing is that they're prepared to hang on to her till she's 18, all being well, and that's a blessing. Far better than being shunted from pillar to post, isn't it?'

I looked at Gary Clark, still trying to take it all in. 'So that's it then? Because of what Kiara disclosed to me, she has been immediately removed and shipped off, no questions asked? Is this how these things work? What if it *had* been a child who was making all this up for some reason? Like you and I discussed this morning, Gary? And, at the risk of sounding like you, how can they be absolutely sure Kiara isn't?'

I was clutching at straws. And daftly so – I didn't want her back with him, ever. I suppose it was just the finality of it all. Gary looked indulgently at me. 'That's hypothetical, and I'm not sure I can answer it, because each case is different. Speaking of which, you make a good point, Casey – we still haven't told you what sealed the deal here. Not properly.'

Which was true. I'd had only managed the briefest of conversations with Gary after he'd sent me the text, and all he'd told me was that social services had indeed spoken to Kiara's mother and that, following that, they'd be taking Kiara into care again as soon as we returned. 'And what did?' I asked.

'A previous conviction that's only just come to light,' he explained.

'For what?'

'For possessing indecent images of children,' he clarified. 'It seems it's not only Kiara's mother who kept a picture library.' He grimaced. 'Seems the two of them didn't so much spy each other over a crowded room as complete a business transaction together.'

'You mean he was one of her *clients*?'

'Back in the day, yes.'

'But, hang on – how did social services not know this? Surely they would have had him police checked?'

'That's a good point, and something currently under investigation, I imagine, but, in essence, it seems Kiara's father had more than one identity. That and some administrative cock-up along the way. Anyway, it was enough to make it clear that any monitoring was an irrelevance – she needed to be taken to a place of safety without delay.'

'So that really *is* that,' I said, sighing deeply. Job done. Problem solved. Criminals being dealt with by the law. Another young life pulled from the brink. Another stolen childhood returned to its rightful owner.

Yet it just felt all so unfinished somehow. I knew we had done the right thing, reporting everything immediately, and there was no question this was the only way for it to end. But I couldn't explain how bereft I suddenly felt. It was like I'd ripped open a part of myself, and I knew that nobody was going to come along and stitch it up.

There was no closure for us as a school, either. Mike explained that other than forwarding on records and finding out which school Kiara would next be attending, our part was over; we wouldn't find out anything else, any more than we would with any other pupil who walked out of our school for the last time. Not if they didn't look back, anyway. Our part in a young life was always destined to be over. That was the nature of a school; that children passed through it.

But at 18, not 12. Oh, I could probably find out more about how things were progressing, if I was vigilant. I imagined that at some point I'd read about both the mother and the father in the local papers, when they'd been to court and sentenced and dragged through the tabloid press, but I wasn't bothered about them. They were horrible human beings, and I didn't actually *want* to hear how they were getting on.

It was Kiara I needed to know about. I wanted to follow her progress, hear about the help she was getting and, most of all, I wanted to know when the day came when she finally realised that what her dad had done to her was wrong. *Then* she would forgive us all, wouldn't she?

Chapter 20

I relayed everything to Mike later that night, as I lay on the couch, unable to eat or concentrate on anything other than my overwhelming sense of guilt. I knew it was irrational guilt but that didn't seem to help.

Mike left his armchair and squeezed in alongside me so he could give me a hug. And a lecture as well. 'Case, I'm sorry, love, but you have to just get *over* it. Don't take this the wrong way, but it's not about you, or how you're feeling. What you did, what everyone did, was the *right thing*. And it doesn't matter if the girl hates you right now, you did it for her. And sometime in the future – even though it may be years ahead yet – she'll understand, and she'll be grateful.'

'I know,' I said. 'I just hate feeling like this. It's like this big cloud is sitting over my head and won't go away. I need a holiday, Mike. Somewhere, hot and dry and warm and entirely cloud-free.'

He rubbed his hand vigorously across the top of my head. 'There,' he said. 'Gone. So now you can snap out of it and stop wallowing in self-pity.'

He nearly got a dig in the ribs for that, but I resisted. Instead I sighed. 'Mike, I'm not *wallowing*, I'm just upset! How can anyone do this job and *not* get upset? I'm serious, I don't know if this job's really for me. This thing with Kiara's really brought it home to me. It's just so emotionally draining.'

Mike snorted in derision. 'Casey, you've been moving towards a job like this for as long as I've known you. Of *course* it's for you. You're good at it and, trust me, you *will* get over it. Bloody hell, love, have you forgotten all the trials of the other kids you've had? Each and every one of them had some horrible past or present.'

'I know,' I said, 'but this is *different*. Almost all the others, so far, are still *in* our school. I get to know the ending. And most of them are relatively happy endings, too. This just feels so unfinished, and it makes me feel ... oh, I don't know how to describe it ... Yes I do, actually. Bloody empty.'

I hauled myself up to a sitting position, tipping him off the sofa in the process. 'Look,' I know you're right,' I said, as I helped him back up. 'I know I have to buck up and shut up. I'm just tired, that's all. Tired and emotional. Perhaps I just need an early night, that's all. And a holiday,' I added, just to press my point home.

He headed off to the kitchen then, and returned clutching half a bottle of red wine we'd had left over from the previous weekend, and two glasses. 'Here we are,' he said, placing the glasses on the coffee table and uncorking the bottle. 'I had a thought. Perhaps that's it. Perhaps you're not quite tired and emotional *enough*.' He handed a glass to me. 'Here, this'll sort you out.'

Though it never seemed like a bright idea to deal with stress at work by necking wine of an evening, one glass does not an alcoholic make, obviously, and I slept like a baby that night. And though it was something of a struggle having to explain Kiara's disappearance to the remaining three members of my current 'team', by the end of the day I was feeling much brighter.

Chloe was, as could have been predicted, inconsolable, but, like me, as the day wore on (and helped enormously by Kelly 'needing' her to help her with the big display board we were making for the end-of-year assembly) even she had managed to dry her copious tears. Life moved on and, somehow, we all had to adjust to it, safe in the knowledge that Kiara was now in the best place.

And now it was Monday, the first day of our week in school, and there was much to be grateful for.

'Miss, miss, we're back home!' was Tommy's excited greeting as I walked up to the school entrance that morning. He'd obviously come to school early and had been waiting outside for me. He looked happier than he had in a long time. 'And guess what,' he continued as he fell into step beside me, doing the hop-skip-and-jump I invariably had to do with Gary. 'Mr Clark has only gone and given me mum a big bag of brand new school uniform for me for next term. I'm gonna look well dapper, aren't I, miss?!'

Ha! I thought. Gary Clark, the old softie. It was usually me that scavenged through all the best second-hand uniform for my Unit kids, and Gary Clark telling me off for being over-generous.

'Did he indeed?' I replied, filing that nugget away for future reference, 'and yes, Tommy, I bet you will look dapper as well. Oh, I'm so happy for you and your mum and sisters, I really am. So you're back in the same house as you were before?'

It seemed the answer was yes, which restored my faith in the powers that be, for it also seemed as if the restraining order that had been slapped on his step-father was working, in that if he so much as went within 'like, a *mile* of us!', as Tommy put it, he would find himself hot-footing it to jail. And it seemed he had heeded the warning. He'd apparently gone back down south and left the family in peace.

Of course you could never say never, and I didn't doubt Tommy's mum still felt scared. But she obviously felt secure enough to stay put, rather than flee again, and that was the best news I could have heard.

And not just for Tommy – for me as well.

'I'm so glad,' I told him as I unlocked my classroom door. 'So even when you move to mainstream classes full time again, I'll still be able to get my Tommy fix here and there.'

He grinned. 'I'm like your coffee, ain't I, miss? Like your caffeine fix!'

'You could be right,' I agreed, sweeping his fringe back from his eyes. I'd changed my mind. It would be a shame to cut that hair.

It would be a shame to say goodbye to him as well – to all of them, in fact. Which meant ends of terms were often particularly emotional times for me, as they often formed natural points on the calendar where a child would move on from the Unit. So despite my resolve to toughen up I knew it would end in tears. Not tears born out of major trauma, God willing, but tears even so.

And they began good and early, first thing on the Wednesday morning, when Jonathan's foster parents came into school with him, to see me – apropos, apparently, of nothing.

'We hoped you wouldn't mind,' Jenny, his foster mum, told me once I'd ushered them into Gary's office. 'Only we just wanted to put a face to a name, really. Jonathan's told us so much about you, and how he's loved his time with you, and we're so pleased to meet you at last, we really are.'

'It's been so helpful for us at home,' Richard, his foster dad, added. 'His behaviour is so much better since he's been in your Unit, and he's really come out of his shell these past few weeks.' He smiled a smile that spoke volumes – of relief, was my hunch. 'We're starting to see the real Jonathan now,' he added, taking his hand and squeezing it. 'And it's lovely.'

Seeing Jonathan hold that hand said it all, really. I thanked them both but pointed out that it wasn't really my doing. 'I really can't take the credit for any of that,' I said, looking at Jonathan, and knowing the hard work would begin in September when he was back in the fray. 'It's this young man here who's done all the hard work. He's made some firm friends and he's been a real pleasure to have. He's a credit to the both of you, he really is.'

I watched them both swelling with pride and I wondered about them. Wondered quite how it must feel to accept a child into your life and bring them up. What must that *feel* like? It must be difficult, I decided – a job not for the faint-hearted – as there would be no physical or emotional bond in place, no foundations to build on either, no instinctive imperative to love and to cherish; how did it feel when they lashed out, pushed you away, defied you, withdrew from you? How did you go from the one place – having a hurt-ing, angry child plopped down in your midst – to the obvi-ous warmth, love and affection I saw before me now? I thought of the Beatles song. Was love really all you needed?

I didn't know, but as I waved them off, Jonathan's hand now in mine, I felt a great rush of respect for them, and also quite tearful. I needed to get a grip on myself, clearly.

There was little or no hope for me come Thursday, however, so I just surrendered myself; I had two six-packs of tissues and what would be would be. The Thursday was the day of our whole school end-of-year assembly – the assembly that everybody loved over all other kinds of assembly. The one where the oldest children, the ones who were leaving us, were very much the stars of the show. This was all about their achievements, the giving out of awards, the teachers standing up to say their various bits and pieces (through veils of tears, obviously) and, usually at this point, they would endear themselves to their pupils even more, by larking about, being generally silly and un-teacherish. Mike Moore would then ramp up the emotional temperature by making one of his fabled 'farewell and good luck' speeches and, though I'd only been at the school for a short while, comparatively, I could tell from watching those who had been there for years and years that it never got any easier to sit through without weeping.

But for all the crying, it was also the happiest of assemblies, with no boring rules being read out, no pupils being singled out for detentions and no talk of lessons and homework. Instead each year group always put on a bit of a performance; usually a song, poem, dance or drama presentation, which soon had everyone's hands red raw from all the clapping.

I was at just such a point, an hour into the assembly, when I was astonished to see Kelly Vickers – who'd inexplicably disappeared from beside me a few minutes back – mounting the stage, followed by Chloe, Tommy and Jonathan. What the hell?

I was bemused not least because we hadn't actually prepared anything. What with everything that had been going on during the last weeks of term, it had kind of disappeared into the 'maybe next time' pit.

But apparently not. 'The children from Mrs Watson's Unit have been working really hard this term,' Kelly was saying, 'and we'd all like to celebrate the end of year by reciting a poem that the kids have worked really hard on. I also need to tell you that this is a surprise for Mrs Watson.' She grinned over at me here. 'We all kept it a *big* secret, so without further ado, I give you ... Chloe, Jonathan and Tommy!'

There was a huge cheer, and heads all around the hall swivelled to smile at me. I reached for my tissues, realising how wily my assistant was – all that sending me away and telling me not to hurry back. It all made perfect sense now. I pulled a second tissue from the pack. I was going to need another of them and fast. How on earth had they managed this, I wondered, catching their eyes, taking in their beams of pure enjoyment. Taking in Jonathan's slight nervousness, Tommy's proud, puffed-out chest, Chloe's air of slight bewilderment at quite what she was doing up there, in front of so many people all at once. And then they began, crystal clear and in perfect unison.

> It's not that we are naughty kids, it's not like that at
>   all,
> The Unit is our place to learn, a place we can walk tall.
> We don't get bullied and we don't feel sad, we work
>   there and we play,
> We learn to cope with everything and we'd just like to
>   say ...
> We're ready now to go to class, and we know that
>   we've improved,
> But sorry, miss, we're staying with you and we shall
>   not be moved!

The cheer that went up then was uproarious. But it seemed they weren't quite done.

> Of course we *know* we have to move, it's time for us
>   to go,
> We just want to say thank you, miss, and that we'll
>   miss you so.

Needless to say, the next bit was a blur. Literally. I was dripping with tears; an emotional wreck. All I remember with any clarity – well, in visual terms, anyway – was Kelly returning to her seat moments later and that, unable to speak due to the lump in my throat, I just did the most unladylike thing I could do. I punched her in the thigh.

And I knew I'd be okay.

Epilogue

I did talk Mike into booking that holiday and, as fate would have it, our fortnight in Menorca marked a watershed for us, being the last family holiday for just the four of us. Boyfriends, girlfriends and other exciting developments put paid to that, but, as any parent will probably attest, in a good way.

As for the children from school, well of course I went back after the holidays ready to face my new challenges, and happily I got to see Chloe, Jonathan and Tommy almost every day. They were back in mainstream classes and each of them went on to do really well. Chloe and her mum got the support they so badly needed, and they thrived on it. So much so that it was decided to hold off looking for a new specialist school for Chloe, particularly when Mrs Jones started to attend AA meetings and, finally, to everyone's delight, stopped drinking. She said that she felt like she'd been woken from a very long sleep. Fingers crossed she doesn't drift away again.

Jonathan continued to live with the Halls, and although he watched other foster children come and go, I found out recently that he remained with them until he was 18, and when he was old enough, he even got sponsored to go to work at Camp America for a full summer, where he assisted in outdoor activities for young people.

Tommy never changed, and I'm glad of it. He did go back to his lessons and he has definitely smartened up some, but his personality dictated that he would for ever be 'class clown'; perhaps the legacy of so many moves and so many new kids to 'get in' with and impress, he just couldn't help himself. Fortunately, however, all the teachers loved him and, bar our delightful Mr Hunt (more of whom later), went out of their way to keep him on the straight and narrow.

I never did hear anything more from Morgan. Her family moved on from that particular travellers' site at the end of that summer, and could have ended up anywhere. And though she was only with us for a short time, I like to think she followed her dreams – and having met Granny Giles, I have no doubt whatsoever that her dad wouldn't have been allowed to stand in her way.

As for Kiara, ah, how much she remained in my heart and on my mind. So much so that when a card was forwarded to me, just before the end of the summer holidays, I burst into tears all over again. I don't know if she was prompted to write it – I liked to think not – but it was just to thank me and say she missed us and wish her friends in the Unit well, and it really meant the world to me.

And, despite her living in a different area and attending a new school, we did receive updates on Kiara's progress fairly regularly, thanks mainly to Gary Clark and his ever-growing list of 'contacts'. He was like a dog with a bone when it came to seeking answers and would pick up that phone every month or so to ask about her progress, just because, like me, what had happened to Kiara had shocked him to the core, despite having already worked for several years in child protection. To have one parent systematically abuse you was trauma enough, but to have two … well, I don't think I'll ever look at the phrase 'out of the frying pan and into the fire' in quite the same way.

I never did find out what sort of sentence either parent served for their crimes, but one bit of positive news did reach me via Gary, a few months later, and it was that Kiara's counselling was apparently going well; that she was beginning to understand that although her mother's behaviour was considered abusive – and it was – what her father had been found guilty of was *far* worse. She remained in foster care and refused contact with her mother when it was offered a couple of years later. I don't blame her. I often think of her now and wonder how she is. That sense of incompleteness never really goes away.

Oh, and as for Mr Hunt – well, what can I say? I'd love to be able to tell you we had a professional discussion about where we needed to differ in our approach to managing kids, and just how dismayed I was that he'd been so needlessly unkind to a child who was already in such a vulnerable place. It never happened.

Instead, picture the scene:

The 'quiet' room, off the staff-room, at the very end of the summer term. Enter Mr Richard Hunt, better known as 'Dick' Hunt, stage right.

Pleasantries are exchanged. Mr Hunt sits at a computer monitor. Mrs Watson, sitting at another, clears her throat, and makes reference to another, similar incident.

CW – So I'd appreciate if you didn't humiliate the students like that. It's both uncalled for and unprofessional. I won't take it any further, I just wanted to let you know how I felt about it.

RH – How *you* feel? How you *feel*? You're not even a real p***ing teacher, so don't try telling me how to do my p***ing job!

CW – Don't you dare speak to me like that! Who the hell do you think you are?

RH – I'm a *real* teacher, love, not a four foot nothing jumped up 'behaviouralist' or whatever the hell you are! Keep out of my damn business, woman, okay?

CW takes a deep breath and does a quick check of the adjacent staff-room.

CW – And you, Mr Hunt, are exactly what all the kids call you behind your back. And a first-class one at that!

Exit, stage left.

TOPICS FOR READING-GROUP DISCUSSION

1. At the end of the book, it's clear that Kiara is caught between a rock and a hard place; she has been exploited by her mother and sexually abused by her father, whom she loves.

   - How do you feel about these characters now?
   - Is there any part of you that sympathises with either of Kiara's parents?
   - Do you agree that it's the right thing for her never to see either parent again?

2. Casey often finds herself struggling with feelings of revulsion and anger towards the adults who have mistreated the children in their care. How do you feel the law currently deals with neglectful or abusive parents? Is it too lenient? Too harsh? Are they victims too?

3. Early in the book, it becomes clear that Kiara has a history of self-harming, but nothing has been followed up. Should a school take more responsibility for such things, or is it always the parents' job?

4. A lot of the children in Casey's 'Unit' are there because difficult home lives make it hard for them to thrive in school. Do you believe schools could and should help to educate parents better?

5. All schools have a Learning Support Department, but not all of them have a designated behaviour manager. This means lots of children slip through the net and get tagged as 'unruly'. Do you think it is important to have a separate unit to work with these children?

CASEY WATSON

One woman determined to
make a difference.

Read Casey's poignant
memoirs and be inspired.

Five-year-old Justin was desperate and helpless

Six years after being taken into care, Justin has had 20 failed placements. Casey and her family are his last hope.

THE BOY NO ONE LOVED

A damaged girl haunted by her past

Sophia pushes Casey to the limits, threatening the safety of the whole family. Can Casey make a difference in time?

CRYING FOR HELP

Abused siblings who do not know what it means to be loved

With new-found security and trust, Casey helps Ashton and Olivia to rebuild their lives.

LITTLE PRISONERS

Branded 'vicious and evil', eight-year-old Spencer asks to be taken into care

Casey and her family are disgusted: kids aren't born evil. Despite the challenges Spencer brings, they are determined to help him find a loving home.

TOO HURT TO STAY

A young girl secretly caring for her mother

Abigail has been dealing with pressures no child should face. Casey has the difficult challenge of helping her to learn to let go.

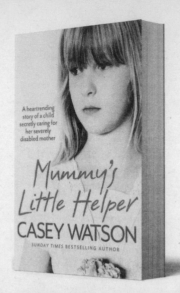

MUMMY'S LITTLE HELPER

Two boys with an unlikely bond

With Georgie and Jenson, Casey is facing her toughest test yet.

BREAKING THE SILENCE

A teenage mother and baby in need of a loving home

At fourteen, Emma is just a child herself – and one who's never been properly mothered.

A LAST KISS FOR MUMMY

Eleven-year-old Tyler has stabbed his stepmother and has nowhere to go.

With his birth mother dead and a father who doesn't want him, what can be done to stop his young life spiralling out of control?

NOWHERE TO GO

What is the secret behind Imogen's silence?

Discover the shocking and devastating past of a child
with severe behavioural problems.

AVAILABLE AS E-BOOK ONLY

Nathan has a sometime alter ego called Jenny who is the only one who knows the secrets of his disturbed past.

But where is Jenny when she is most needed?

NO PLACE FOR NATHAN

Jade and Scarlett, seventeen-year-old twins, share a terrible secret.

Can Casey help them to come to terms with the truth and rediscover their sibling connection?

SCARLETT'S SECRET

Moving Memoirs

Stories of hope, courage and the power of love...

If you loved this book, then you will love our Moving Memoirs eNewsletter

Sign up to...

- Be the first to hear about new books

- Get sneak previews from your favourite authors

- Read exclusive interviews

- Be entered into our monthly prize draw to win one of our latest releases before it's even hit the shops!

Sign up at

www.moving-memoirs.com

Harper True.

Time to be inspired

Write for us

Do you have a true life story of your own?

Whether you think it will inspire us, move us, make us laugh or make us cry, we want to hear from you.

To find out more, visit

www.harpertrue.com or send your ideas to **harpertrue@harpercollins.co.uk** and soon you could be a published author.